W0369985

Contents

Unit 1 Australia

○* 1 Welcome to Australia! ▸ pp. 6–7

Read Judith's blog on p. 6 of your student's book and complete the sentences below in your own words. Then add a sentence each to give more information.

1 From the plane window Judith felt very small and a bit scared because she saw how huge and empty Australia was. The outback looked flat and endless.

2 When Judith landed in Melbourne, she got a shock because in Cologne it was a warm summer day and in Australia a cold day in winter.

3 School in Melbourne is different from school in Cologne for the following three reasons: The school year in Australia has 4 terms. The Australian students are into school from 8.30 - 3.00. After that there are lots of extracurricular activities. School fills the whole day.

4 During a five-day hike in the bush a snake fell out of a tree onto another girls arm.

5 In their free time lots of Australian teenagers do sports. They also often celebrate parties on during the weekends.

Now you

Write notes about what you have learned from Judith's blog. Make two lists about: 1) Australia; 2) teenagers in Australia. Compare your notes with Germany and teenagers in Germany. Write two paragraphs about the differences in your exercise book.

1 Australia: is huge; flat, beautiful landscape; red earth

2 Teenagers in Australia: 4 school terms; school until 3.15 pm; learn how to surf.

○ 2 REVISION Describing a picture ▸ p. 7 • SF (p. 126)

Look at picture 3 on p. 7 of your student's book. Why does it look strange? What's happening? Describe details of the scene in a paragraph. Use **in the foreground/background/middle, on the left/right**, *etc.*

Picture 3 shows a man on a beach in Australia. He is dressed as Father Christmas, but he's wearing shorts, T-shirt and flipflops because it's summer. The man is in the foreground in front of the Christmas tree that is in the middle of the picture. Under the tree there are presents in colorful papers. (gold, silver, red). Father Christmas is decorating (putting) a star on the top of the tree. In the background we can see the sea. There are sea

INFO BOX

On beautiful Seventy-Mile Beach on Fraser Island (east coast) you can drive your car, jeep or bus or even land a small plane.

*○ leichte Übung

Test

3 Australia quiz ▸ pp. 8–9

a) Read pp. 8–9 of your student's book again. Then mark A, B or C. You need the letters in brackets in b).

1 The capital of Australia is …

A	B	C
Melbourne. (P)	Canberra. (G)	Sydney. (D)

2 The first Europeans landed in Australia in the … century.

A	B	C
14th (G)	15th (I)	16th (E)

3 In 1788 the British founded a colony for …

A	B	C
farmers from Britain. (L)	convicts from Britain. (R)	pilgrims from Britain. (E)

4 Australia was founded in …

A	B	C
1770. (S)	1788. (T)	1901. (B)

5 Today most immigrants to Australia come from …

A	B	C
the USA. (O)	Asia. (I)	Britain. (E)

6 A big health problem for the people of Australia is …

A	B	C
pollution in the cities. (M)	the ozone hole. (I)	dangerous animals. (E)

7 Australia's population is mainly of … origin.

A	B	C
American (E)	Asian (I)	European (O)

8 Which three animals are found only in Australia?

A	B	C
Kangaroo, emu, lion. (U)	Koala, emu, kangaroo. (A)	Koala, kangaroo, lion. (L)

9 The Great Barrier Reef is … long.

A	B	C
more than 2,000 miles (O)	1,500 km (H)	more than 2,000 km (S)

10 The Great Barrier Reef has about … species of corals.

A	B	C
200 (P)	400 (N)	1,500 (A)

b) If your answers are correct, you can put the letters in the brackets in the right order to give you the name of a group of people: Aborigines

4 LISTENING Captain James Cook ▸ p. 9 • WB (p. 77) 2

a) Listen carefully and write T (true) or F (false).

1 James Cook had six brothers and sisters. F

2 Cook became a sailor like his father. ____

3 He joined the Royal Navy[1] when he was 27. ____

4 He was sent by the British government to discover an unknown southern continent. ____

5 He made his first journey in a ship named the *Resolution*. ____

6 He claimed Australia for Britain on his second journey. ____

7 He was killed on a Hawaiian island. ____

WB, pp. 54–57

0304

b) Listen again and take notes (important dates, events). Use your notes to write a short biography of Cook's life. Write about 100 words in your exercise book.

[1]Royal Navy [ˌrɔɪəl ˈneɪvi] *königliche Marine*

* schwierige Übung

5 REVISION The emu (Simple present) ▸ p. 9

Complete the text about emus with the correct form of the verb in brackets.

The emu lives (live) only in Australia. It belongs (belong) to the family of flightless birds, so it doesn't fly (not fly). Emus run (run) very fast, up to 50 km an hour. They eat (eat) most things, including flowers, small snakes and frogs. The emu drinks (drink) a lot of water and enjoys (enjoy) playing in water too. Wild emus don't live (not live) longer than ten years, but in animal parks they live (live) much longer.

0405

6 STUDY SKILLS Charts ▸ p. 11 • SF (p. 127)

Write about the two charts. What kind of charts are they? What do they show? What can you conclude? Use phrases from your student's book (p. 10).

1 Reasons for visiting Australia (international visitors)

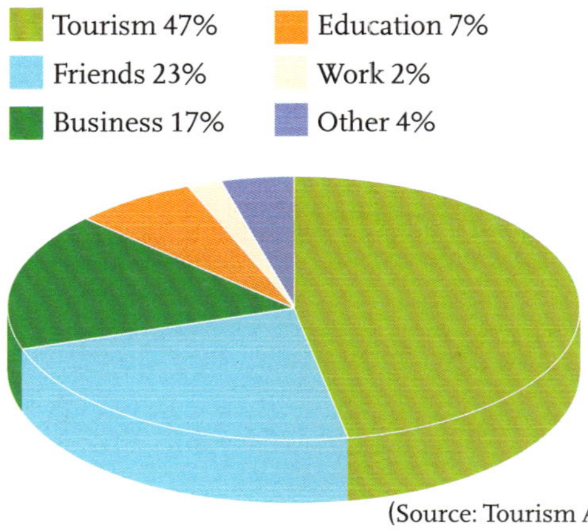

(Source: Tourism Australia 2009)

2 Where visitors to Australia come from (in thousands)

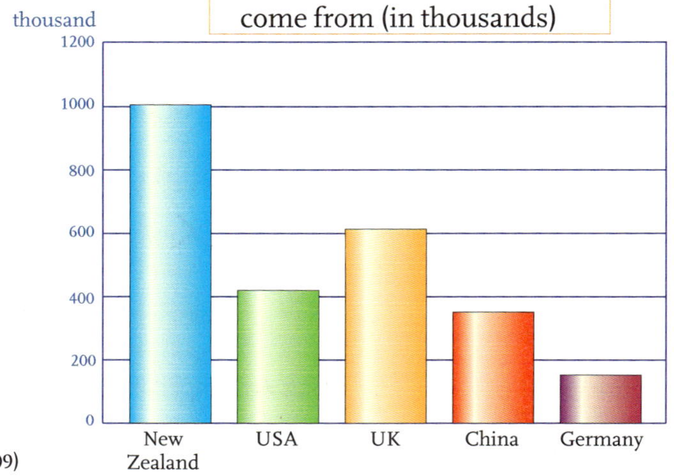

1 This is a ________ chart. It is divided into six sections which show what percentage of international visitors go to Australia and for what reasons.

2 This is a ________

7 WORDS More than one meaning ▸ p. 11

What do the underlined words mean in the following sentences? Write the German translation.

1 A Change at gate 5. B Where can I change money? C Aborigines changed the landscape.

A umsteigen B ______ C ______

2 A Space isn't a problem in Australia. B Move on two spaces. C The Great Barrier Reef can be seen from space.

A ______ B ______ C ______

3 A Do you have a £10 note? B He sings the high notes very well. C Take notes.

0507 A ______ B ______ C ______

8 REVISION First trip to Australia (Past perfect) ▸ p. 14

Complete the sentences with the words in brackets. Use the past perfect.

Lucy was going to Australia. She had already bought (already buy) a ticket to Sydney. She was very excited because she ______ (not be) to Australia before and her best friend ______ (tell) her how fantastic it was. She wanted to visit so many places that she ______ (read) about, including the outback. She also wanted to see the Great Barrier Reef because she ______ (hear) a lot about it. She ______ (not see) corals close up, so she wanted to do a diving[1] or a snorkelling trip. She hoped that she

0508 ______ (save) enough pocket money to do all those things.

9 PRONUNCIATION Same sound, different spelling ▸ p. 14 3

The words have the same vowel sound but different spellings. Complete the words, then listen and check with your CD.

1 [uː]: em_u_ kangar___ f___ l___se contin___

2 [ɜː]: l___rn w___d d___t s___f s___vice j___rney

3 [eɪ]: gr___t ___ght w___ve r___n p___

0509 4 [iː]: r___f l___ve bel___ve l___gal k___

[1] dive [daɪv] *tauchen*

10 SPEAKING COURSE Part 1: Hi! (Having a conversation)

p. 14 • WB (p. 80) 4

a) Look in your student's book again (p. 14). Write phrases you could use in the different steps of a conversation. More than one phrase is possible.

Step 1: You want to start a conversation with somebody you don't know.

Hello! / Excuse me, … / Hi! / …

Step 2: You introduce yourself.

By the way, my name's … • How are you? • Good to meet you

Step 3: You start with a few general questions.

Have you ever …? • Have you … yet? • What about you?

Step 4: You ask for help or information.

Can you tell me …? • Do you know where …?

Step 5: You tell someone that you don't understand, or you ask someone to repeat something.

Sorry, I didn't get that. • Sorry, can you say that again, please? • The/A …? • What's that? • What does that mean?

Step 6: You end the conversation.

Bye! • See you tomorrow. • Thanks for your help.

> **INFO BOX**
>
> There are many words and expressions that are unique to Australia. One is 'fair dinkum', which means 'real, true, genuine'. You will often hear the expression 'a fair dinkum Aussie', – a true Australian.

b) Ben is a student from the UK. It's his first day in Sydney. He wants to go to the beach, so he asks a girl on the street where he can buy some things that he needs. Complete the conversation with phrases from a). Then listen to your CD (4) and check your answers. The CD gives only one possible answer.

Ben Hi! Excuse me, …

Girl Hi! Going to the beach?

Ben Yes, but it's a bit too hot for me. (By the way), my name's Ben.

Girl Hi, Ben! I'm Lucy. Nice to meet you. You're from the UK, right?

Ben Yes, I am. I live near London. Where do you live? Are you from Sydney? Are you from here?

Girl Sure. I've lived here all my life. It's a great city.

Ben This is my first day here. Can you tell me where I can get some sunscreen? I can get some sunscreen and a hat? I didn't think it would be so hot.

Girl Well, there's a place that sells tourist stuff just round the corner on the left. Then you can slip, slop, slap.

Ben Sorry, I didn't get that. Can you say that again please, please?

Girl (*laughing*) Well, that's just what we say here – because of the sun: 'Slip! Slop! Slap!'

Ben Oh. Well, Thanks for your help. Bye!

WB, pp. 68–69

0610
0611

c) Write a new dialogue between Ben, who now wants to rent[1] a bike for the day, and a girl he meets on the beach. Use phrases from the six steps in a) and ideas from b).

[1] rent [rent] *mieten*

11 WORDS Get it right! ▸ p. 15

Choose the correct word from the boxes and use it in the correct form to complete the sentences.

1 | go • drive • ride |: Jeannie lives in the middle of nowhere, so she can't go anywhere by train or bus. She rides her horse and her dirt bike every day, but will she ever learn to drive a car?

2 | do • make • take |: Rob does lots of sport. He goes surfing almost every day, but just now he's taking a break because he has to work hard for school. At the moment he's making breakfast before he goes to the beach with his books.

3 | than • as • when |: Jeannie learned to ride a bike as a small child, when she was only three. I think riding a dirt bike is more fun than playing cricket.

4 | while • during |: During school time Jeannie talks to her teachers and classmates on her webcam. She can do her school work on her laptop while she's sitting under a tree.

5 | need • take |: Jeannie says the nearest town is 300 miles away. How often do they need to go there and how long does it take to get there?

0711

12 EVERYDAY ENGLISH WRITING (Writing an e-mail) ▸ p. 15 • WB (pp. 81–82)

Test

You would like to know more about the sports that Australian teenagers play. Write to Rob and ask questions. Here are some notes. Tell him about popular sports in Germany too. Write your e-mail in your exercise book. Use paragraphs and topic sentences and think of a good closing sentence.

Skydiving – how learn? expensive? how dangerous?
Surfing – how long to learn? equipment expensive?
Cricket – school sport? rules?
Aussie rules football – how different?

Dear Rob,
I found your website really interesting and your pictures are great.
I'd like to know more about …

WB, pp. 63–67

Now you

What are the advantages and disadvantages of living 'in the middle of nowhere' like Jeannie? Write notes in your exercise book and prepare a three-minute talk for class.

Ideas: free • clean air • quiet • close to nature[1] • animals • boring • not many friends • no entertainment

[1] nature ['neɪtʃə] *Natur*

13 REVISION They don't like you to do it (Verb + object + *to*-infinitive) ▸ *p. 18 • WB (p. 83)*

*Make one sentence out of two. Use the underlined words and make sentences with verb + object + **to**-infinitive.*

1 Tourists shouldn't climb Uluru. The Aborigines don't like it.

The Aborigines *don't like tourists to climb* Uluru.

2 Visitors can ask questions about Aboriginal traditions. Aboriginal tour guides like that.

Aboriginal tour guides *like visitors to ask* questions about Aboriginal traditions.

3 All white people should respect Aboriginal culture. The Aborigines want that.

The Aborigines *want all white people to respect* Aboriginal culture.

4 Tourists shouldn't take photos of some special parts of Uluru. Tour guides ask this.

Tour guides *ask tourist not to take* photos of some special parts of Uluru.

5 Visitors to Uluru should do as the warning signs say. The national park guides expect it.

0813 The national park guides *~~want~~ expect the visitors to Uluru to do* as the warning signs say.

14 REVISION She didn't know what to do (Question word + *to*-infinitive) ▸ *p. 18 • WB (p. 83)*

*Complete the text with a question word (what, who, how, where, which) + **to**-infinitive.*

When Lena Müller arrived at Alice Springs airport, her au pair family hadn't arrived. She waited half an hour and she didn't know *what to* do. It would be best to phone, but she didn't know *how to* use public phones in Australia, and she didn't have any Australian change anyway. She thought she might take a bus but she didn't know *which* bus *to* take and she wouldn't know *where to* get off anyway. She wondered *who to* ask for help. Maybe she could ask the woman at the information desk, but she didn't know *how to* explain the situation in English. Suddenly, a voice behind her said, 'Hey! You must be Lena. Sorry we're late. We had a problem with a dangerous snake in our yard and we didn't know *where to* look for it. We're not sure where it is now … But no worries,

0814 we'll show you *what to* do if you see it …'

15 WORDS Linking words ► p. 19

a) With linking words you can join words, phrases and sentences and make your ideas easier to follow. Write a list of the linking words that you already know: **and, or, but** ... after, when, as/while, of because, although, if, so that, before, so

b) Now use linking words to complete the text about Uluru.

Although it stands in the middle of the hot Australian desert, Uluru or Ayers Rock is visited by thousands of tourists from all over the world. The best way to get there is to fly to Alice Springs, but you can also make the long, dry journey by road through the outback.

Before you go to Uluru, it's a good idea to find out what to do and what not to do there. When visitors first see Uluru they are amazed at its size and beauty. Uluru is an unbelievable sight at any time of day, but the best time is sunset if you want your visit to be a magical experience. Tourists stand in wonder[1] while the rock changes from all colours of red and orange to deep blue.

Because of their beliefs the Aboriginal people don't like visitors to climb Uluru, so instead of climbing the rock tourists usually walk round it. But there are still visitors who climb it. Some visitors do the climb although they are not fit enough. So far more than 30 people have died of a heart attack as (while) they were climbing in the hot sun.

0915

16 WORDS What do they mean? ► p. 19

a) Explain these words. Use relative clauses with **who, which/that** *or* **where**.

sleeping bag: A sleeping bag is something that you sleep in when you are camping.

sunscreen: __________

desert: __________

teenager: __________

ancestor: __________

orphan: __________

b) Use at least four words from a) in two or three sentences.

When you go on a camping trip in the Australian desert, you need

0916

[1] wonder ['wʌndə] *Staunen*

17 What to do in Alice Springs (*to*-infinitives instead of relative clauses) ▸ p. 19 • WB (p. 83)

*Make the sentences shorter with a **to**-infinitive instead of a relative clause.*

1 There are some really good tours that you can choose from. ... good tours *to choose from.*

2 There are lots of interesting places that you could visit. ... places ______

3 There are some good hotels that you could stay at. ... good hotels ______

4 There are miles of fascinating outback that you can drive through. ... outback ______

1017 5 There are so many new things that you can discover. ... new things ______

18 MEDIATION
Climbing Sydney Harbour Bridge (Spoken English to German) ▸ p. 19 • WB (p. 79) 5

a) *You are going to climb Sydney Harbour Bridge with your parents. You call the Bridge hotline to find out answers to your parents' questions. Take notes in your exercise book.*

1 Wie kommt man am besten zur Brücke?
2 Kann man mit dem Auto hinfahren?
3 Gibt es eine Vorbereitung?
4 Wann müssen wir dort sein?
5 Wie lange dauert der Aufstieg?
6 Gibt es Dinge, die wir tun sollten oder nicht tun dürfen?
7 Was soll man anziehen?
8 Was geschieht, wenn das Wetter schlecht ist?

WB, pp. 70–71

b) *Answer your parents' questions in German.*

19 WORDS Word families ▸ p. 19

a) *Write another word that belongs to the same word family. Write **N** (noun), **V** (verb) or **A** (adjective). Sometimes your new word may have the same form as the word given.*

comparison (N)	*compare (V)*	race (*dt. Rasse*, N)	(racist (A))
protect (V)	(protection, protective (A))	respect (V)	(respect (N))
reaction (N)	(react (V))	connect (V)	(connection (N))
conclude (V)	(conclusion (N))	contrast (N)	(contrast (V))

b) *Use words from a) in the correct form and complete the text.*

For 60 years thousands of children of mixed (races) were taken from their Aboriginal families because of the government's (racist) policy[1]. The stealing ended in 1970, but the government did not say sorry. The Aborigines (reacted) with sadness and anger[2]. For years they (concluded) that the government was not sorry. The government did not apologize officially until 2008, but in (contrast) to earlier years, Aboriginal culture and traditions are now more (respected) by the white population.

1019

[1] policy ['pɒlɪsi] *Grundsatz* [2] anger ['æŋgə] *Wut*

20 STUDY SKILLS Reading literature

▸ pp. 24–25 • SF (pp. 138–139)

a) These words are important when you talk about literature. Find the correct definition and match.

plot	the main people in the story
setting	comparisons and metaphors to create atmosphere
atmosphere	the action and events that take place in the story
characters	the place where and the time when the story takes place
imagery	the feeling created by the setting of the story

b) In what ways can an author present his/her characters to the reader? Read p. 25 of your student's book again. Then write a short paragraph. Use your own words.

The author can chose between many ways. He may describe them or show the reader what they are like through their language and way of speaking, their actions, feelings, thoughts, words and their connections to other characters.

21 READING WORKING WITH THE TEXT In the outback

▸ pp. 20–25 • WB (pp. 77–79)

a) Put the events of the story in your student's book (pp. 20–24) in the correct order.

Rusty the dog disappears.	
Bill repairs the Dog Fence where an emu has hit it.	
The Flying Doctor is called to fly Bill to hospital.	
A black boar attacks Bill and Rusty and hurts them badly.	
Bill and Colm drive into the Victoria Desert.	1
Colm shoots the boar.	
Colm helps Bill by filling holes made by wombats.	
Colm finds Rusty and helps Bill to save her.	
Colm takes Bill and Rusty in the car to the cattle station to get help.	

WB, pp. 58–62

b) Creative writing. Write a new story with its setting in the Australian outback in your exercise book. Use the pictures and the following ideas:

Two teenagers rent[1] a jeep and drive into the outback. They find a strange map that is marked with a cross ... They want to find out what it means ...

1122
1123

[1] rent *mieten*

Skills Check 1

1 LISTENING Summer vacation 6

You will hear a conversation between Dan and his sister Mel. Read the questions first, then listen and tick A, B or C. You will hear the recording only once.

1 The conversation takes place …
- A on a train to Brisbane.
- B on a plane to Melbourne.
- C on a bus to Darwin.

2 Their arrival time is …
- A 4.45.
- B 14.45.
- C 14.54.

3 Why are Dan and Mel going there?
- A To go to summer camp.
- B To do a summer job.
- C To visit family.

4 Mel and Ruth are …
- A friends.
- B sisters.
- C cousins.

5 During their vacation Dan and Mel are planning to …
- A go shopping.
- B do lots of sport.
- C do lots of sightseeing.

6 They have already been to the City Museum …
- A twice.
- B three times.
- C four times.

2 LISTENING A day in the life of … 7

You will hear part of a radio interview with two firefighters from the Queensland Fire Service. Read the questions below first, then listen to the recording. You will hear the recording twice.

a) *What do you hear about in the interview? Tick the correct box.*

- ☐ A koala rescue operation
- ☐ The history of bushfires in Queensland
- ☐ Why bushfires start

b) *Tick true or false.*

		True	*False*
1	Bob has been a firefighter for 30 years.	☐	☐
2	Steve had an office job with a company before he became a firefighter.	☐	☐
3	On average, Queensland gets 258 days of sunshine a year.	☐	☐
4	In the fire season firefighters work round the clock and get very little sleep.	☐	☐
5	Bob flies a helicopter with waterbombing equipment.	☐	☐
6	Natural causes of bushfires are high temperatures and strong winds.	☐	☐
7	Eucalyptus forests burn easily because of the oil[1] in the leaves.	☐	☐
8	The public can't do anything to prevent bushfires.	☐	☐
9	It's often difficult to make people leave their homes, although the fires are close.	☐	☐
10	The worst bushfires in recent[2] years were in Queensland in 2009.	☐	☐
11	Bob remembers saving a little girl's cat from the garden of her ruined house.	☐	☐
12	Steve really likes being a firefighter.	☐	☐

[1] oil [ɔɪl] *Öl* [2] recent ['riːsnt] *jüngst, aktuell*

3 READING Sydney for everyone

a) Look at the text quickly. What is it about? Tick a box.

☐ Sydney's beaches ☐ Sydney's history ☐ Sydney's sights

b) Look at the text a second time. What information does it give? Tick the correct boxes.

☐ Opening times ☐ Prices ☐ Sights information ☐ How to get there

SYDNEY FOR EVERYONE

Start at The Rocks

The Rocks is the oldest part of Sydney. Historically, it is an area of great importance as it is here that Sydney was founded, when the first British convicts were sent here in 1788. Because of its well-preserved architecture from colonial times, it is often called Sydney's 'outdoor museum'. But today The Rocks combines historic buildings with trendy boutiques, souvenir shops, cafés, restaurants and a weekend street market. The Sydney Visitor Centre is here too, so it's a good place to start your visit. **Open** daily from 9.30 am to 5.30 pm.

Climb Sydney Harbour Bridge

This is one of Sydney's most popular tourist attractions, called the Coat Hanger by local people. It's easy to see why. Don't miss the challenge of the Bridge Climb for an unforgettable experience! The building of the bridge took about eight years. It was opened in 1932 and is used by about 150,000 vehicles daily. It takes about 80,000 litres of paint to paint the bridge once, and painting never stops. Did you know that the movie star Paul Hogan, better known as 'Crocodile Dundee', used to be a bridge painter before he became famous? **Opening times**: 7 am to 8 pm daily.

Visit Sydney's historic buildings

Visit Elizabeth Farm in Parramatta, Australia's oldest European building. Begun in 1793, the farm was the home of John and Elizabeth Macarthur, settlers from England who became sheep farmers and started Australia's wool export industry. The old house, its furniture and its gardens show visitors how they lived in the early 19th century. There are no guided tours. **Open** 9.30 am to 4 pm Fri. to Sun.

See a world-famous sight

The spectacular Sydney Opera House is situated in Sydney Harbour, surrounded by water on three sides. It was built by a Danish architect and was completed in 1973. Its design is a masterpiece of twentieth-century architecture and a world-famous sight. By the way, not only opera but also concerts, theatre and ballet are performed here. If you take the two-hour backstage tour, you can stand on the stage where stars like Pavarotti or Michael Bublé have performed, and find out stories from behind the scenes ... Oh, and be prepared to climb up 300 steps!

Visit Sydney Aquarium

Sydney Aquarium is one of the biggest in the world, with at least 6,000 fish, mostly Australian, and 650 different species. Don't miss the collection of sharks[1]. Some weigh as much as 300 kg. Visitors walk through underwater viewing tunnels to see marine life close up, so you can look a shark in the eye! **Opening times:** 9 am to 10 pm daily.

[1] shark [ʃɑːk] *Hai*

READING

c) *Now read the text for details. Is the information true (T), false (F) or not in the text (N)? Tick the correct box.*

		T	F	N
1	The Rocks is an area of Sydney which reminds[1] visitors of Australia's colonial history.	☐	☐	☐
2	Pilgrims from Britain arrived there in 1788.	☐	☐	☐
3	There is a Rocks farmers' market on Fridays.	☐	☐	☐
4	Painting the Harbour Bridge is a never-ending job.	☐	☐	☐
5	The Macarthurs were cattle farmers from England.	☐	☐	☐
6	People call John Macarthur 'Father of the wool industry'.	☐	☐	☐
7	Sydney Harbour Bridge was started in 1924.	☐	☐	☐
8	The Bridge is a railway bridge only.	☐	☐	☐
9	Sydney Aquarium is home to 6,000 species of fish.	☐	☐	☐
10	Sydney Aquarium is the world's second biggest.	☐	☐	☐
11	Sydney Opera House is near Sydney Harbour on a small island.	☐	☐	☐
12	A Danish architect designed and built Sydney Opera House.	☐	☐	☐
13	You can also see theatre productions at Sydney Opera House.	☐	☐	☐
14	The backstage tour is one of the most popular tours.	☐	☐	☐
15	The backstage tour is not suitable[2] for people who can't climb.	☐	☐	☐

WRITING

4 WRITING A blog or a summary

Complete task a) or task b).

a) *Write an interesting blog in English about your first day sightseeing in Sydney. You can take some facts from the text 'Sydney for everyone', but use your own words (about 150 words). Remember your writing skills.*

23 December

Hi, folks!

Yesterday I arrived in this most fantastic city! Here I am in …

[1] remind [rɪˈmaɪnd] *jm. an etw. erinnern* [2] suitable [ˈsuːtəbl] *geeignet*

b) *Write a summary of the following story in about 150 words in your exercise book.*

A birthday surprise

It would be Nina's birthday soon. Her brother David and some friends had planned a birthday surprise for her – a trip to Kakadu National Park.

The group left early on their drive, laughing, joking and talking about what they might do there, walking, rock-climbing, fishing, swimming in a freshwater billabong[1], picknicking by the river.

'You must be joking! What about the crocs?' said David, who was always careful and never did anything dangerous.

Cathy said that most of the crocs in the park were freshwater crocs, smaller and not aggressive like 'salties'.

Mike argued that thousands of visitors went to Kakadu, but only two or three died each year in a croc attack. But Mike loved an adventure. He never said no to anything scary.

'I agree,' said Nina, who had always been the wild one in the family. 'The park authorities take visitor safety seriously. Rangers check for crocs, even by helicopter. They can see them easily in the clear water. David, don't spoil[2] our fun! You're always scared of something. Enjoy yourself more! I always say: No risk, no fun!'

'So they've closed Twin Falls Gorge[3] and a few other places for swimming for no reason, have they? Why do you think there are crocodile warning signs everywhere? Nobody can give you a guarantee[4] that there will be no salties in the area, not even the rangers. There are no guarantees,' David continued in a serious voice.

'Come on, guys, that's enough. No more arguing. It's Nina's birthday tomorrow, and we're going to have a great time, eh, Nina?' said Mike laughing.

The rest of the day went well. In the evening they celebrated Nina's birthday round a campfire at the campsite. Nina was really happy.

The next day they made the short trip to the famous Jim Jim Falls. Nina wanted to see the beautiful plunge[5] pools. It was hot, and Mike was looking forward to a swim in the cool, clear water. The way there was a difficult climb over rocks. Mike and Nina loved rock climbing, so they soon left the others behind.

Suddenly David noticed that the two had disappeared. Nervously he shouted their names, but they were nowhere. 'This is crazy,' said David. 'We said we would all stay together.' Just then David fell and hurt his foot.

Cathy tried to calm him down, but she was worried too. 'They'll be back soon. We'll just wait here. You can't climb rocks anyway, if your foot hurts.' But after two hours Mike and Nina still hadn't come back. David felt sick with fear. The minutes seemed like hours. The waiting went on …

'Hey, you lazy guys! Where were you? It was great up at the plunge pool!' shouted a familiar[6] voice at last. It was Mike. They were back. David threw his arms round his sister. Nina didn't say much …

Safely back home after the trip, when she was alone with David, Nina said, 'David, I have to tell you about what happened up at the falls. A huge saltie suddenly appeared on the edge[7] of the lower pool only ten metres away. I was terrified, Mike too – but he would never admit[8] it. I couldn't move at first, but the croc came closer, so fast. We just dropped our stuff and ran away over the rocks – lucky that salties are bad climbers. We were too scared to go back, so we had to wait until it had gone – the worst two hours of my life. We could both have been eaten alive if we had jumped in the water. I'm so sorry about – you know. You were right – there are no guarantees. And David, please don't tell Mum and Dad …'

[1] billabong *Seitenarm eines Flusses* [2] spoil [spɔɪl] *verderben* [3] gorge [gɔːdʒ] *Schlucht* [4] guarantee [ˌgærən'tiː] *Garantie* [5] plunge [plʌndʒ] *Tauch-* [6] familiar [fə'mɪlɪə] *vertraut* [7] edge [edʒ] *Kante* [8] admit [əd'mɪt] *zugeben*

5 SPEAKING Travelling 8

a) At a travel agency in Australia you ask about tours to Uluru for your family. Listen and speak to the assistant: ask questions or form sentences in the pauses.

Assistant G'day! How can I help you? ...

1 Grüße ebenfalls und frage, was man bei der Uluru-Tour alles sehen kann.
2 Frage, wann die Tour losgeht.
3 Frage, wie lange die Tour dauert.
4 Frage, ob die Fremdenführer Aborigines sind.
5 Frage, ob man auf der Tour Frühstück bekommt.
6 Frage, wie viel die Tour kostet und was im Preis inbegriffen ist.
7 Sage, du möchtest die Tour für zwei Erwachsene und zwei Jugendliche für morgen buchen.

b) Describe picture A or B: the background, the colours, the atmosphere. Say what the persons in the pictures are doing and how they maybe feel. Talk for about three minutes.

A

B

I'd like to talk about picture A ...

c) If you went to Australia, would you prefer to see the outback or to have a beach holiday? Say why. Talk for two minutes. You can record what you say.

6 MEDIATION Berlin tours

An Australian student would like to go to Berlin for a weekend and he asks you what you can see there. You find a brochure about Berlin tours. Write down the most important things for him in English in your exercise book.

Entdecken Sie Berlin mit Alpha Tours – wann und wie Sie wollen

Genießen Sie eine geführte Tour mit dem Bus, Fahrrad oder zu Fuß zu den vielen Sehenswürdigkeiten der Hauptstadt. Wir organisieren Touren jeder Art für große und mittlere Reisegruppen sowie für kleine Gruppen von 8 bis 12 Personen – und das jeden Tag! Wählen Sie Ihre spezielle Tour aus unseren vielen Angeboten aus!
Entdecken Sie u.a. folgende Highlights: **Regierungsviertel, Berliner Reichstag, Brandenburger Tor, Checkpoint Charlie, Mauerreste, Museumsinsel, Fernsehturm, Kaiser-Wilhelm-Gedächtniskirche, DDR Museum, Berliner Dom, Potsdamer Platz, Schloss Charlottenburg.**

Wir bieten:
- moderne klimatisierte Reisebusse, neue bequeme Stadträder.
- Vormittags-, Nachmittags- und Abendtouren mit sämtlichen Eintrittsgeldern inklusive.
- genug Zeit für Fotostops und Erfrischungspausen bei allen Touren.
- bei Ganztagstouren ist auch ein Mittagessen enthalten.
- erfahrene, kundige Stadtführer/innen, die mehrere Fremdsprachen sprechen.

Besuchen Sie unsere Website, um Tourbeschreibungen, Preisinformationen, Adressen unserer Filialen und vieles mehr in Erfahrung zu bringen. Rufen Sie uns an oder kommen Sie ganz einfach vorbei!
Tel.: 030-529 487–0 / www.alphatoursberlin.com

How did you do?

Check your answers to the exercises on p. 87. Then answer the questions below with Yes or No.
If you tick No or would like some extra practice on that point, go to the exercise in your workbook (▸ pp. 54–76).

1 LISTENING Summer vacation	Yes	No	Exercise
1 Hast du dir vor dem Hören die Fragen gründlich durchgelesen?	☐	☐	▸ 1, 2
2 Hast du die Detailfragen ohne Probleme beantworten können?	☐	☐	▸ 3, 4
3 Konntest du die Sprecher mühelos verstehen?	☐	☐	▸ 6
2 LISTENING A day in the life of…			
1 Konntest du nach dem 1. Hören beurteilen, um welches Thema es im Interview geht?	☐	☐	▸ 1, 2
2 Hast du dir beim 1. Hören Notizen gemacht (Zahlen, Daten, Namen)?	☐	☐	▸ 3, 5
3 Konntest du den australischen Akzent mühelos verstehen?	☐	☐	▸ 7
4 Konntest du dem Sprechtempo mühelos folgen?	☐	☐	▸ 8
3 READING Sydney for everyone			
1 Konntest du schnell herausfinden, um was es in dem Text geht?	☐	☐	▸ 10, 16a
2 Hast du nach Schlüsselwörtern (*key words*) gesucht, um Antworten zu finden?	☐	☐	▸ 11
3 Konntest du die Antworten auf Detailfragen problemlos finden?	☐	☐	▸ 13, 14
4 Hast du die Bedeutung unbekannter Wörter erschließen können?	☐	☐	▸ 15, 16b
4 a) WRITING A blog			
1 Hast du deine Ideen mithilfe eines *brainstorming* gesammelt und dazu Notizen gemacht?	☐	☐	▸ 17
2 Hast du einige der 5 Ws am Anfang deines Textes berücksichtigt?	☐	☐	▸ 18
3 Hast du Informationen aus Exercise 3 benutzt und mit eigenen Worten beschrieben?	☐	☐	▸ 31, 32
4 Hast du passende Adjektive für deine Beschreibungen benutzt?	☐	☐	▸ 35
5 Hast du hauptsächlich das *simple past* benutzt?	☐	☐	▸ 30
6 Hast du deine Wortstellung (z.B. in Nebensätzen) überprüft?	☐	☐	▸ 37
7 Hast du *linking words*, z.B. *but, after, before, while, because, although, so* benutzt?	☐	☐	▸ 32, 33
8 Hast du deine Rechtschreibung/Grammatik überprüft und deine Fehler korrigiert?	☐	☐	▸ 38
4 b) WRITING A Summary			
1 Hast du die wichtigsten Ereignisse erkannt und dazu Notizen gemacht?	☐	☐	▸ 17
2 Hast du die 5 Ws am Anfang deiner Summary berücksichtigt?	☐	☐	▸ 18
3 Hast du die wichtigsten Ereignisse mit eigenen Worten wiedergegeben?	☐	☐	▸ 19, 31, 32
4 Hast du direkte Rede sowie Beschreibungen weggelassen?	☐	☐	▸ 19a+b
5 Hast du den Unterschied zwischen dem *simple present* und *present progressive* beachtet?	☐	☐	▸ 29
6 Hast du deine Wortstellung (z.B. in Nebensätzen) überprüft?	☐	☐	▸ 37
7 Hast du *linking words*, z.B. *but, after, while, because, although, so* benutzt?	☐	☐	▸ 32, 33
8 Hast du deine Rechtschreibung/Grammatik überprüft und deine Fehler korrigiert?	☐	☐	▸ 38
5 a) SPEAKING Travelling			
1 Hast du problemlos passende Fragen mit *do/does* oder mit Fragewörtern bilden können?	☐	☐	▸ 23
2 Hast du in den Pausen schnell genug die passenden Fragen stellen können?	☐	☐	▸ 25b
3 Hast du die notwendigen Vokabeln gewusst?	☐	☐	▸ 24a
5 b) SPEAKING Travelling			
1 Hast du bei der Bildbeschreibung Ortsangaben wie z. B. *on the right/left* usw. benutzt?	☐	☐	▸ 24
2 Hast du Dinge, die die Personen gerade tun, mit dem *present progressive* beschrieben?	☐	☐	▸ 29
3 Hast du die Atmosphäre der Bilder mit passenden Adjektiven beschrieben?	☐	☐	▸ 25, 35
4 Hast du wichtige Vokabeln für die Bildbeschreibung gewusst?	☐	☐	▸ 24a
6 MEDIATION Berlin tours			
1 Hast du beachtet, mit eigenen Worten nur das Wesentliche weiterzugeben bzw. nicht alles wörtlich zu übersetzen?	☐	☐	▸ 26
2 Hast du (falls nötig) für unbekannte Wörter Umschreibungen benutzt (*paraphrasing*)?	☐	☐	▸ 34

Unit 2 The road ahead

1 WORDS Planning the road ahead ▸ *pp. 32–33*

***a)** Read pp. 32–33 of your student's book again. Find collocations and match the words below.*

work | pass | inherit | become | have | make | get | graduate | start

exams | hard | a millionaire | qualifications | from university | a fortune | kids | a career | a difference

1801

***b)** Look at the pictures of Marcia, Andy and Trish taken six years after the young people left school. Which road did they take? Imagine what they say about their past, present and future. You can use phrases from a).*

Marcia

Andy

Trish
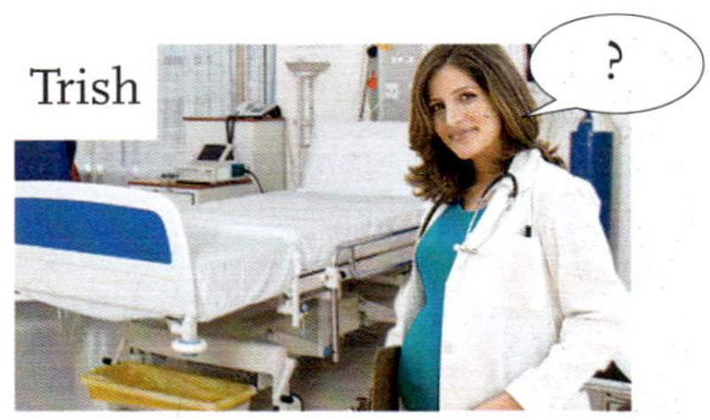

Marcia: *Well, I took the career road. I worked hard at school,*

Andy: *I decided against a career. I didn't go to university, but*

Trish: *I always planned to become a doctor, and I did. But I found the right partner and now* I'm pregnant. I love my job but I look forward my first child much more. It'll be nice to spend lots of time into our little family. But of course it's also nice to can help the ill people ~~and~~ to get healthy.

***c)** What are the advantages of planning your 'road ahead'? What are the disadvantages? First make notes using phrases from a). Then write a paragraph in your exercise book.*

2 WORDS Personal qualities ► p. 36

a) What kind of person are you? What do others think? Choose words from the boxes and make sentences.

a bit • quite • very • (not) always • sometimes • usually

annoying • calm • careful • confident • energetic • flexible • funny • good at ... • hard-working • helpful • honest • interested in ... • keen on ... • likeable • musical • nervous • noisy • organized • practical • punctual • quiet • relaxed • reliable • serious • sporty • tidy

1 I think my friends would describe me as ______________________

____

2 I think my family would describe me as ______________________

____

3 Maybe my teachers would say I'm ______________________

____

b) If an interviewer said to you 'Tell me about yourself', how would you answer? Think carefully. Don't be too confident, but don't hide your good qualities. Prepare your answer in a few sentences. Write in your exercise book.

1902

3 REVISION Luke's dad wants him to ... (Infinitive constructions) ► p. 36 • WB (p. 83)

a) Luke doesn't really know what he wants to do next year. What do other people want him to do?

1 Dad 'Stay on at school and go to university.'
2 Mum 'Work hard and get good A-levels.'
3 Brother 'I think you should do volunteer work abroad for a year.'
4 Girlfriend 'Stay at home and get a job in a bank.'
5 Best friend 'Follow your dream and become a racing driver!'

1 Luke's dad wants *him to stay on at school and go to university.*

2 His mum expects ______________________

3 His brother told ______________________

4 His girlfriend wants ______________________

5 His best friend told ______________________

b) Look at Luke's questions on the right. Then complete the sentences with a question word + to-infinitive.

1 What shall I do next year?
2 When shall I leave school?
3 What kind of job shall I train for?
4 Whose advice[1] shall I take?

1 Luke doesn't know *what to do next year.*

2 He can't decide ______________________

3 He doesn't know ______________________

1903 *4* He doesn't know ______________________

[1] advice [əd'vaɪs] *Rat, Ratschlag*

4 SPEAKING COURSE Part 2:
Excuse me, ... (Asking for, confirming and giving information)

▸ p. 37 • WB (pp. 80–81) 🎧 9, 10

a) ***Asking for information./Being polite.*** *How could Jonas sound less direct, more polite and more friendly? Rewrite his sentences. There is more than one suitable answer.*

1 Jonas: Hello. I want to go to Windsor. How do I get there?

Excuse me. I'd like to go to Windsor. Do you think you could/Could you tell me how to get there?

2 Jonas: Hello. Where can I get a bus to Windsor?

____

3 Jonas (*in train*): Can you close the window?

____

4 Jonas: I want to do a tour of the castle. When does the next tour leave?

____

5 Woman (*in train*): Are you on holiday here? Jonas: Yes. __________

Woman: And did you enjoy the tour of the castle? Jonas: Yes. __________

Woman: Have you been to London before? Jonas: No. __________

b) ***Confirming information.*** *Listen to the conversation at the train station (🎧 9). Which phrases does Elias use to confirm the information he is given? Find seven more phrases and write them down.*

Is that right?

____

c) ***Giving information.*** *Amina is having a phone interview for a summer job with a tour company in London. They need someone to answer telephone enquiries[1] from German tourists in German.*

WB, pp. 68–69

1 First listen carefully (🎧 10) to part of Amina's telephone interview.

2004

2 Now it's your turn to be interviewed. Listen to the interviewer's questions (1–5) and give suitable answers in the pauses. You can take ideas from Amina's interview. Remember to be polite.

[1] enquiry [ɪn'kwaɪəri] *Anfrage*

5 Extra Blue box: Word building Interview tips (Negative prefixes) ▸ p. 37, p. 178

Complete the interview tips with the negative form of the adjective in brackets. Guess or check the meaning of any word you don't know in your dictionary. You can also use your dictionary to find out which negative prefix you need.

1 Interviewers don't like applicants to be *unpunctual* (punctual). If you're going to be late, call the company and say why. It's very *impolite* (polite) to arrive late without an explanation.

2 While you're waiting, you often have to fill in a form. Do it as well as you can, even if you think it asks for *unnecessary* (necessary) information. Write clearly. Most interviewers find *illegible* (legible) handwriting extremely annoying. Don't give *incorrect* (correct) or *inexact* (exact) information.

3 Answer all the interviewer's questions, even if you think some of them are *unimportant* (important) or *irrelevant* (relevant).

4 Think carefully before you speak. If you have to give reasons, never use *~~un~~ illogical* (logical) arguments.

5 Don't be negative about any part of the job description. The interviewer may think you're *inflexible* (flexible) or even *unable* (able) to do the work.

6 Remember, if the interview goes badly, don't feel *unadequate* (adequate). You were just *unlucky* (lucky).

2105

6 Blue box: Same verb, different meaning ▸ p. 40, p. 181

a) *Some students are talking about their interview experiences. Complete what they say with a **to**-infinitive or a gerund.*

1 I'll never forget ______ (go) to my first interview. I was terrified.

2 I almost forgot ______ (say) 'thank you' before I left.

3 I went on ______ (talk) about my hobbies for ages. Not a good idea!

4 I knew I was doing OK when the interviewer went on ______ (talk) about money.

5 I tried ______ (change) the subject when the interviewer asked a question I couldn't answer.

6 I wish people would stop ______ (tell) me what to do!

b) *What do you remember doing in the past? What must you remember to do next week? Write three sentences each in your exercise book.*

2106 *I remember falling off a horse when I was eight./I must remember to buy concert tickets next week.*

7 STUDY SKILLS Writing a formal letter

▸ p. 41 • SF (p. 146)

a) *Complete the information about formal letters.*

1 If you start a formal letter with 'Dear Sir/Madam,' you usually end it with '____________________'.

In AE you may begin with 'To ____________________' and end with '____________________'.

2 If you know the name of the person, you start with '____________________' + name and end with

'____________________' (BE) or just '____________________' (AE).

b) *You are planning to do a language course in Oxford for three weeks during your summer holidays. Someone has given you the address of a nice place to stay. Write a formal letter to the house owner, Ms Claire Harris, 8 Broad Street, OX 13 AP. For help you can use the phrases in the box and your student's book (p. 146). Write in your exercise book or use a computer.*

1 Tell her what you would like (room with breakfast, maybe evening meal)
2 Give the dates of your stay.
3 Ask questions (how much it would cost per week, etc.)
4 Tell her a little about yourself (your level of written/spoken English, what kind of person you are, interests).

> …
> I am planning to do a language course in Oxford and need accommodation for three weeks from … to …, if possible with … •
> I would be grateful if … •
> I am … years old and have studied English for … years …
> My level … • I look forward …
> …

WB, pp. 63–67

8 WORDS Looking ahead

▸ p. 41

Complete the text with words from the box.

application • apply for • candidate • CV • education • employers • enclose • placements • qualifications • résumé • university

Whatever road ahead you take, you'll need some qualifications. Maybe you'd like to go to ____________ for a few years, or you may decide to ____________ a job or volunteer work. Whatever you do, when you send your ____________ you must ____________ your ____________, which the Americans call '____________'. This gives future ____________ information about your school ____________ to date and any ____________ you have had. If you are an interesting ____________, you may be invited to an interview. Then it's up to you!

2208

9 REVISION After school (Gerund as subject and object) ▸ p. 42 • WB (pp. 83–84)

Complete the sentences with your own ideas. Use gerunds.

1 When I leave school I'll really enjoy listening to music

2 Visiting Paris is something I've always wanted to do.

3 Learning at school is very important for kids our age.

4 I can't really imagine leaving my homecountry forever

2309 5 I prefer going to university so that will be important when I apply for a job.

10 REVISION A newspaper ad (Gerunds after prepositions) ▸ p. 42 • WB (p. 84)

First, match the adjectives to the prepositions that follow them (green boxes). Then complete the job advertisement below with the words from the green boxes and the pink box. Think carefully. Sometimes there is more than one possibility.

tired | bad | good | interested | used | keen | afraid

of | at | on | in | to

travel and make foreign contacts • organize • set up a new project • do routine work • make decisions[1] • work alone • miss a great opportunity

Join us as our new PROJECT MANAGER

We are a leading London IT company looking for someone who ...

- is tired of doing routine work.
- is bad at working alone
- is good at organizing
- is interested in traveling and making foreign contacts
- is used to making decisions
- is keen on setting up a new project

If you are afraid of missing a great opportunity

call Sam Fletcher on 02072 455325 for more details.

2310

Now you

Think about your future possibilities. What are you keen on? What are you good at? What are you bad at? What are you used to? What are you not interested in? Write at least one sentence as an answer to each question in your exercise book.

[1] decision [dɪ'sɪʒn] *Entscheidung*

11 MEDIATION US high school programs

▸ p. 43 • WB (p. 79)

Test

You would like to participate in an American high school program, but your parents aren't too happy about it. You found this information on a website. Tell your parents the important facts in German. Make notes in your exercise book first.

An academic year at an American high school

Who can apply?
If you are a foreign student 15 to 18 years of age, you may apply for a place in the academic program of an American high school. You should have good school grades and a good level of everyday English. All applicants will be interviewed in their own country, where they will also take a test in English.

School programs
US school classes start in August and finish in June. You will choose your schedule from a wide range[1] of academic subjects which include Math, English, Science, US History, Business, Economy, Industrial Design and PE. Additionally, you will choose extracurriculars. These may be different from school to school, but will usually include sports, music, drama, voluntary[2] social work and environmental projects. Your school will expect you to take part in all aspects of high school life.

What does the program price include?
You will stay with an American host family and will study at a local high school, often together with students from your host family. On arrival in the US you will be met at the airport and will be taken to your host family. You will have your own room and will eat with the family in the evenings and on weekends. The program price also includes your school registration fees[3] and educational school trips.

What extra costs will I have to pay?
Not included in the price are application fees, your travel/flights to the US, your travel insurance, medical insurance[4], transport to and from school, school books and school lunches.

WB, pp. 70–71

12 WORDS Word families

▸ p. 44

Complete with a word from the same family as the word in brackets. If you need a verb, use the correct tense.

Simon had read an advertisement (advertise) for a summer job with a sports company. He decided to send an application (apply) to the manager, who invited him to an interview.

On the day of the interview, Simon dressed suitably (suitable) and arrived on time. He saw that there were six other applicants (apply) for the job, but he tried not to be nervous. The manager asked Simon about his free-time activities (active) and he seemed to be very interested (interest). Simon showed that he was an organized (organize) and energetic (energy) person who loved sport. The manager also asked Simon about his strength (strong) and weaknesses (weak).

Simon hopes that he was able to impress (impressive) the manager and that he will be the succesful (success) candidate.

2412

[1] range [reɪndʒ] *Auswahl* [2] voluntary ['vɒləntəri] *freiwillig* [3] registration fee [ˌredʒɪ'streɪʃn fiː] *Anmeldegebühr*
[4] medical insurance [medɪkl ɪn'ʃʊərəns] *Krankenversicherung*

13 LISTENING Phone calls ▸ p. 45 • WB (p. 77) 11

Test

Mrs Holby is a busy manager. Ben, her assistant, writes the times of her appointments and interviews in an appointments diary. Listen to the telephone calls, and write the necessary changes in the diary.

Monday	Tuesday	Wednesday	Thursday	Friday
~~10.30 Interview Ms Jane Morton~~	10.15 Mr D. Thomas, (Bell Electronics)	8.30 Dentist's appointment	9.30 Presentation	8.30
		11.00 Interview Ms Maria Langton		
	2.30 Interview Mr Peter Marlow		2.30 Visit to MPR Software, Harrow	2.00 Interview Mr S. Rogers

WB, pp. 54–57

14 WORDS Word building (Nouns from verbs) ▸ p. 45

a) *How do you make nouns from the following verbs? Write the nouns in the correct list. If you are not sure, use your Dictionary (SB pp. 195–236).*

advertise • argue • announce • assess • confuse • decide • delay • discuss • elect • experience • interest • introduce • react • revise • segregate • work

Same form as the verb	-sion	-tion	-ment
work	discussion	election reaction	advertisement
interest	confusion	introduction	argument
experience	decision	segregation Trennung	announcement
delay Verzögerung	revision	discussion	assessment

2514

b) *Choose five nouns from a) and use them in five sentences.*

1 ______

2 ______

3 ______

4 ______

5 ______

15 READING WORKING WITH THE TEXT
How to be a teenage millionaire

▸ pp. 46–48 • WB (pp. 77–79)

a) Put the events of the story (SB pp. 46–47) in the correct order. Write numbers 2–8 in the boxes.

She bought the address whateverlife.com with the money. .... ☐

Ashley started to design websites when she was nine years old. *1*

She got her first cheque from an advertising company. .... ☐

Her mother lent her $8 to buy a domain name. .... ☐

Big advertising companies started to get interested in her website.... ☐

She wants to study design in her dream city, New York. .... ☐

She left school before her 16th birthday. .... ☐

She had a problem with a friend who was working for her. .... ☐

INFO BOX

A UK teenage millionaire
In 2002, when he was only 14, Fraser Doherty from Edinburgh started earning lots of money – in the kitchen. He used his grandmother's secret recipe[1] to make healthy jam[2] without sugar. Everybody loved it, so he decided to sell it at a local market for extra pocket money. Soon he had to rent a factory and employ people to make it. Now he sells his famous jam in large supermarket chains throughout the UK.

b) What do you know about Ashley? Tick the correct answers.

1 She's determined and ambitious. ☐

2 She earns money by selling her designs. ☐

3 She doesn't miss school. ☐

4 She believes in herself. ☐

5 She has a strict set of rules for people who work for her. ☐

6 She's artistic and hard-working. ☐

7 She lives the normal life of a teenager. ☐

8 Her business brings in about $7,000 a month. ☐

c) If Ashley was in your class, how would you and your classmates probably feel about it? Answer the questions in a few sentences each. Give reasons for your answers. Write in your exercise book.

1 Would Ashley be a classmate just like all the other classmates?

I think class relations would be just the same. First, .../I don't think Ashley would really be the same as other classmates. One reason is that ...

2 Would you want to work for Ashley? Why (not)?

I don't think it would be good to work for somebody in your own school class. The main reason is that .../ Yes, maybe ...

3 Ashley would be different from all your other classmates because of her money. Do you think this might lead to problems in the class?

WB, pp. 58–62

Yes, maybe. Being Ashley's friend might divide the class into two groups .../No, I don't think this would lead to problems ...

d) **Extra** *Do some internet research to find another teenage millionaire and describe how he/she started a business. Maybe you can find parallels to Ashley's story. Write notes in your exercise book. Then tell the class about the teenage millionaire's story.*

2616 2617

[1] recipe ['resəpi] *Kochrezept* [2] jam [dʒæm] *Marmelade*

How well can you do these things?	Very well	OK	Practise!
LISTENING AND READING SKILLS: I can …			
… understand longer conversations and longer written texts, e.g. *In the outback* (SB pp. 20–24).	☐	☐	☐
… understand and find detailed information from what I hear or read, e.g. details about Ashley's business (SB pp. 46–47).	☐	☐	☐
… understand the Australian accent without difficulty, e.g. Rob talking about sports (SB p. 13).	☐	☐	☐
SPEAKING AND WRITING SKILLS: I can …			
… start and continue a conversation on an everyday topic with someone I don't know.	☐	☐	☐
… ask, confirm and give information in English.	☐	☐	☐
… ask and answer typical questions at a job interview.	☐	☐	☐
… write my CV with the correct format.	☐	☐	☐
… write a formal letter of application and a formal letter asking for information, in a suitable style and format.	☐	☐	☐
MEDIATION SKILLS: I can …			
… report the most important facts from conversations or written texts, both from German into English and from English into German.	☐	☐	☐
… use synonyms or paraphrasing for words and phrases I don't know.	☐	☐	☐
TOPICS: I have learned …			
… about Australia's geography, history, animals, natural sights (the outback, Uluru, the Great Barrier Reef), the School of the Air, the Flying Doctor Service.	☐	☐	☐
… about Aboriginal culture and history, e.g. 'the Dreaming' and 'the stolen generations'.	☐	☐	☐
… how to talk about work experience and qualities needed for different jobs.	☐	☐	☐
… how to write a job application and present myself at an interview.	☐	☐	☐
STUDY AND LANGUAGE SKILLS: I know …			
… how to use an English grammar.	☐	☐	☐
… how to create visual aids and use them in presentations.	☐	☐	☐
… how to talk about, write about and compare statistics, using tables, bar charts and pie charts.	☐	☐	☐
… how to talk about plot, setting, atmosphere and characters in literary texts.	☐	☐	☐

HOW I COULD IMPROVE MY ENGLISH SKILLS: I could …

(e.g. work through parts of Skills Check 1 again, revise the unit vocabulary lists …)

____

____

Skills Check 2

LISTENING

1 LISTENING First day at work 12

You are going to hear Jenna talking about her first summer vacation job. Read the task first, then listen and tick A, B or C. You will hear the recording twice.

1 Jenna got her first summer vacation job in a ...

- A clothes store.
- B shoe store.
- C designer jeans boutique.

2 She wanted to work there because ...

- A she loves shoes.
- B she couldn't get any other job.
- C the store sold shoes for teenagers.

3 Jenna got the job there because ...

- A she had work experience.
- B they needed someone quickly.
- C she was the only applicant.

4 The first customer[1] bought shoes in ...

- A brown and black.
- B black and blue.
- C blue and brown.

5 The customer paid ... for two pairs of shoes.

- A 155 dollars
- B 310 dollars
- C 410 dollars

6 Jenna didn't know the correct price because ...

- A someone told her the wrong price.
- B there was no price on the shoes.
- C the price on the box was wrong.

7 When Jenna couldn't find shoes for the second customer, she ...

- A asked the manager.
- B showed the customer different shoes.
- C waited in the store room[2] until the customer had gone.

8 Jenna thought it would be unprofessional to ...

- A say she couldn't find the shoes the customer wanted.
- B ask how the system in the store room worked.
- C hide in the store room.

READING

2 READING Jobs

a) *Look at the five texts quickly. What are they about? Tick a box.*

Young people describing a job they would like to do ....

Young people describing work experience that they have done ....

Young people describing jobs that they do ....

b) *Read what the young people say. Look at the pictures on the next page. Which picture matches which description? Write A–F in the boxes. There is one picture more than you need.*

1 I work outside half of the time. I don't mind because there's usually something going on. And we work in twos on the street, so there's always a partner to talk to. We are often called to a traffic accident, a fight or a robbery in the area. I prefer it to sitting in the office writing up reports, but we have to do that too. There's some routine, but my job is much better than a nine-to-five job, and it's surprising how much crime there is in a small town. We're always busy. It's never boring.

2 I love my job, though it isn't easy. You have to work really hard, and the pay is not good. We work shifts. I often have the night shift, which is quite hard because you're mostly alone, so it's difficult if there's an emergency. I always hope nothing will happen when I'm doing a night shift. We have to know a lot. It's a very responsible job and we mustn't make mistakes. We have to be exact in our work, punctual, reliable, caring and always friendly to our patients.

[1] customer ['kʌstəmə] *Kunde/-in* [2] store room *Lager*

3 In my job you have to be calm and organized and you have to be good in a team. I work with my boss and his partner. I always have to be punctual and reliable, but that's no problem. I had to learn a lot and do exams, and I'm still training, so I don't do operations myself yet. I'm glad that we can help old ladies and children when their pets are ill. But we also help farm animals, cows, sheep, horses. You don't have to mind getting your hands dirty. It's a good feeling being able to help and save lives.

4 I'm an outdoor person. I definitely couldn't work in an office all day sitting at a desk and looking at a computer. I work for a company in town, but our projects are everywhere in the area, sometimes they're really big projects, office blocks or industrial parks. My job isn't very nice in winter when it's cold and it rains a lot. You have to be fit and quite strong. We carry heavy[1] building materials and we start early. It's nice to look at a beautiful new building and know that you were part of it.

5 This is my second year as a trainee. It's hard work and I had to start from the bottom, cleaning floors and preparing vegetables – pretty boring. At first I learned all the standard dishes that are always on the menu, but I really enjoy being artistic with food and creating my own dishes. I hope to have my own restaurant one day.

A
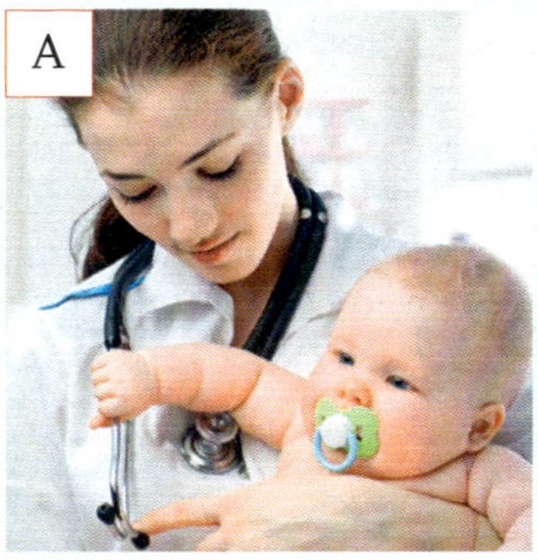
Lauren

B
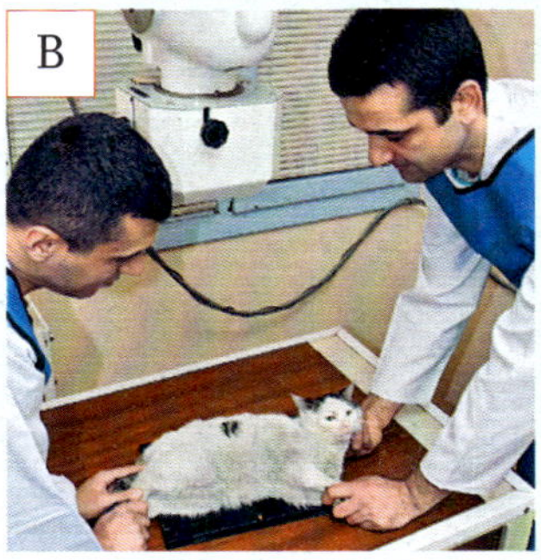
Adam

C

Penny

D

Lucy

E

Nick

F

Sam

c) Write the correct name.

1 Who would like to own his own business? ______

2 Who likes being part of a big project? ______

3 Who doesn't like working night shifts? ______

4 Who spends about 50% of working time outdoors? ______

5 Who has completed one year of training? ______

6 Who assists at operations? ______

7 Who hates office work? ______

8 Who does heavy work and has to be fit? ______

[1] heavy ['hevɪ] *schwer*

3 WRITING A formal letter

An English friend sends you an advert from the Cornish Daily Post advertising holiday jobs in hotels in Cornwall. You are interested and would like more information. Write a formal letter to the manager and ask about the following:

- *what kind of hotel work is available*
- *where the hotels are*
- *hours, pay, free time*
- *accommodation, meals.*

Give information about yourself. Say why you would like to work in Cornwall, when you would be free and how many weeks you would like to stay. Write about 120 words. Make notes below, then write the letter on the computer.

Holiday jobs in Cornwall

We have a number of jobs for German-speaking students who would be interested in working in our hotels for 6–8 weeks in summer.
Please send your application with CV in English to:
George Sutton
Cornish Hotels
139 Sutton Road
Bude, EX23 OBA

4 WRITING Your CV

Now write your CV to send with your application. Think about which information to include (personal and contact details, education, qualifications/skills, etc.). Present the information in a logical order. Remember to include a short personal statement. Make notes below, then write your CV on the computer.

CURRICULUM VITAE

5 WRITING An informal letter

Write an informal letter to your English friend telling him/her that you have applied for a job in Cornwall. Say why the job interests you and think about positive and negative things. One good thing may be that you could visit your friend in Cornwall. Brainstorm your ideas first (mind map, list). Write about 150 words in your exercise book.

WRITING

6 SPEAKING Jobs and work experience

a) *Look at the pictures and describe the jobs. Compare the advantages and disadvantages of the two jobs. What are the people doing? How do you think the people feel when they're doing these jobs? Which job would you prefer? Why? Make notes in English and talk for about three minutes.*

1

2

b) *Prepare answers to the following questions, so that you can speak freely and confidently. Talk for about three minutes. You can record your speech.*

- Why do you think work experience is important for young people?
- Do you have a weekend job or an after-school job?
- Talk about any work experience that you have. What did you like about it and what didn't you like?
- What would you like to do when you leave school? Go to university? Spend time abroad? Train for a job?

7 MEDIATION Small ads

You have met an American student. She doesn't know much German but would like to have a job for a few hours a day. You find some suitable jobs in the local newspaper. Make notes in English first so that you can tell her about the jobs. Use your exercise book for your notes.

1 **Café am Brunnen**

Aushilfe gesucht für ca. 3 Stunden vorm. od. nachm.
Arbeiten in Küche und Café (z. B. Gemüse putzen, Küche aufräumen, Tische decken u. abräumen). Servieren von Eis und Kuchen im Gastgarten.
Gute Bezahlung.
Tel.: 793 501

2 **Hotel am Domplatz**

Für die Rezeption suchen wir **ab sofort** eine Kraft mit sehr guten **Englischkenntnissen.** Aufgaben: telefonische Auskunft u. Betreuung ausländischer Gäste. Erfahrung in der Hotelbranche erwünscht, aber nicht Voraussetzung. Halbtags od. stundenweise als Aushilfe.
Überdurchschnittliche Bezahlung.
Tel.: 482 502 (Fr. Lenz)

3 **Englischsprachige Kinderbetreuung**

für amerikanische Familie gesucht (Kinder 2 und 4 J.).
Mo–Fr, 13–17 Uhr. Keine Arbeit im Haushalt.
Führerschein nicht erforderlich.
Tel.: 602 335

4 Student/in für **englische Konversation** gesucht.
Mo u. Do vorm. je 2 Std. (Gruppe 6 Pers.)
2. Gruppe Di u. Fr möglich, **native speaker** willkommen! Deutschkenntnisse nicht erforderlich. Tel.: 496 395 (Vera)

Well, there's a job in a café. You have to ...

How did you do?

Check your answers to the exercises on p. 88. Then answer the questions below with Yes or No. If you tick No or would like some extra practice on that point, go to the exercise in your workbook (▸ pp. 54–76).

	Yes	No	Exercise
1 LISTENING First day at work			
1 Hast du dir beim 1. Hören Notizen gemacht (z.B. Zahlen, Farben)?	☐	☐	3, 5
2 Konntest du den amerikanischen Akzent mühelos verstehen?	☐	☐	6, 7, 9
3 Hast du dem Sprechtempo problemlos folgen können?	☐	☐	8, 9
2 READING Jobs			
1 Konntest du schnell herausfinden, um was es in den Texten geht?	☐	☐	10, 16a
2 Konntest du Antworten auf die Detailfragen problemlos finden?	☐	☐	11–13
3 Hast du die Bedeutung unbekannter Wörter erschließen können?	☐	☐	15, 16b
3 WRITING A formal letter			
1 Hast du auf eine geeignete Form geachtet (z.B. *addresses, date*)?	☐	☐	21b
2 Hast du eine passende Gruß- und Schlussformel benutzt?	☐	☐	21a
3 Hast du deine Fragen (direkt und indirekt) mühelos bilden können?	☐	☐	23, 36
4 Hast du deine Rechtschreibung/Grammatik überprüft und deine Fehler korrigiert?	☐	☐	37, 38
4 WRITING Your CV			
1 Hast du alle erforderlichen Informationen in einer passenden Reihenfolge präsentiert?	☐	☐	22a+c
2 Hast du ein kurzes *personal statement* geschrieben?	☐	☐	22b
3 Hast du deine Rechtschreibung/Grammatik überprüft und deine Fehler korrigiert?	☐	☐	37, 38
5 WRITING An informal letter			
1 Hast du eine passende Gruß- und Schlussformel benutzt?	☐	☐	20
2 Hast du deinem Text eine Struktur gegeben?	☐	☐	20
6 SPEAKING Jobs and work experience			
1 Hast du mit dem *present progressive* beschrieben, was die Personen gerade machen?	☐	☐	29
2 Hast du mit passenden Adjektiven die Jobs beschrieben?	☐	☐	35
3 Hast du die erforderlichen Vokabeln für die Bildbeschreibung gewusst?	☐	☐	24a, 35
7 MEDIATION Small ads			
1 Hast du beachtet, mit eigenen Worten nur das Wesentliche weiterzugeben bzw. nicht alles wörtlich zu übersetzen?	☐	☐	26, 27
2 Hast du (falls nötig) für unbekannte Wörter Umschreibungen benutzt (*paraphrasing*)?	☐	☐	34
3 Hast du modale Hilfsverben richtig benutzt (*can, have to, needn't* usw.)?	☐	☐	28

Unit 3 Life in the big city

1 Pros and cons of city life ▸ pp. 50–51

a) *If you live in a city or big town, answer these questions in a paragraph. Write in your exercise book.*

Which city/big town do you live in? Do you make full use of what your city has to offer (culture, entertainment, sports events, shopping, libraries)?
Which aspects of city life do you really enjoy? Which aspects of city life would you like to improve?

b) *If you live in a small town or a village, answer these questions in a paragraph. Write in your exercise book.*

Which is the nearest city to your town or village? How often do you and your family/friends go there? Why do you and your family/friends go there (work/school, entertainment, sports events, airport, doctors, shopping, libraries, etc.)? What do you like about the city? What don't you like? Name a few advantages and disadvantages of city life.

c) *Which of the following are problems of cities in your country? Which problems do you think are more serious in developing countries? Write a few sentences in your exercise book.*

waste disposal, clean drinking water, epidemics, traffic noise, crime, violence, pollution, no jobs

d) *What is the message of the text 'A world of cities?' on p. 50 of your student's book? How does the message make you feel? Write a paragraph in your exercise book.*

2 Background File: Hong Kong ▸ p. 52

a) *Complete the timeline of Hong Kong's history. Use information from p. 52 of your student's book. Use the simple present.*

1821: *British merchants start to use Hong Kong Harbour for their opium trade in China.*

1842: ______________________

1898: ______________________

1984: ______________________

1997: ______________________

b) *In your exercise book, make a list of tourist activities in Hong Kong which are named on p. 52 of your student's book. Would you like to visit Hong Kong? What would interest you most?*

3 WORDS Describing things and places in the city

▸ p. 55

a) *Which words do not fit? Mark the adjectives that you would not generally use to describe the nouns given. Then add two suitable adjectives to each list.*

1 ... skyscrapers: shiny, ancient, huge, ______

2 a/an ... shopping mall: expensive, busy, polluted, popular, ______

3 the public transport system: crowded, clean, financial, cheap, ______

4 a/an ... financial centre: international, rural, world-famous, modern, ______

5 a/an ... suburb: poor, rich, modern, crowded, official, clean, quiet, ______

b) *Write sentences about Hong Kong from the information and pictures on pp. 52–54 of your student's book. Use suitable adjective and noun combinations from a).*

1 *There are lots of shiny, huge skyscrapers in Hong Kong.*

2 ______

3 ______

4 ______

3503 5 ______

4 EVERYDAY ENGLISH LISTENING Getting from the airport

▸ p. 55 13

Test

a) *Sophia and her parents have just arrived at Hong Kong Airport. Sophia asks about transport into town at the info desk. Listen to the conversation once and answer the questions in note form. Then listen again to check your answers.*

1 Which part of Hong Kong do Sophia and her parents want to go to? *Hong Kong Island.*

2 If they go by taxi, which colour taxi should they take and why? ______

3 How long is the journey by Airport Express train? ______

4 What does a train ticket cost per person? ______

5 How often do the trains run? ______

6 When does the first train leave from Central Station? ______

7 What are the advantages of going by Airport Express if you have an early flight back home?

______

______

______

WB, pp. 54–57

b) *At the hotel, Sophia asks for information. Write a short dialogue between Sophia and the man at reception[1]. She asks the following:*

- if there's a free hotel bus to the airport from the hotel (yes)
- what time the bus leaves for early flights (6.30 am)
- how long the journey takes (about 45 minutes)
- where the bus drops passengers at the airport (Arrivals terminal)

[1] reception [rɪˈsepʃn] *Rezeption*

5 Background File: Johannesburg ▸ p. 56

Test

a) *Are the statements true or false? Mark a letter.*

	True	False
1 A short, popular name for Johannesburg is 'Jozi'.	F	A
2 The discovery of gold first made Johannesburg South Africa's economic centre.	A	S
3 Sandton is a poor suburb with a high crime rate.	J	N
4 Apartheid meant strict segregation laws for black and white.	K	R
5 The main reason for the Soweto Uprising was the bad conditions[1] in black schools.	T	A
6 There were no equal rights for black people until the 1990s.	R	A
7 The anti-apartheid fight lasted[2] for 29 years.	P	A
8 Nelson Mandela was elected first black president of South Africa in 1994.	S	A
9 Today Johannesburg's main problems are a very high crime rate and AIDS.	I	F

b) *If the letters you have marked are correct, in the right order they spell the name of one of the eleven official languages in South Africa:* Africaans

6 REVISION A city of contrasts (Participle clauses instead of relative clauses) ▸ p. 59 • WB (p. 85)

a) *Rewrite the sentences with participle clauses instead of the relative clauses.*

1 Around 1900 Johannesburg grew rapidly because of the thousands who were looking for gold.

Around 1900 Johannesburg grew rapidly because of the thousands looking for gold.

2 Today Sandton is maybe the suburb which is most visited by tourists.

3 Tourists who stay in big hotels in Sandton may think people who live in Johannesburg are lucky.

4 In contrast, anyone who visits Soweto will be shocked by the picture that is presented there.

5 In Soweto babies who are born with AIDS make up over 30 percent of all births.

3606

INFO BOX

Johannesburg is one of the world's most important business centres for gold and diamonds. Almost half the world's gold is found in the area.
Johannesburg is also very green. People say there are more than 10 million trees in and around the city!

[1] condition [kən'dɪʃn] *Bedingung* [2] last *dauern*

7 WORDS What goes together? (Participles as adjectives) ▸ p. 59

Make compound adjectives from the two boxes and match them to the noun groups. Read the noun groups first.

1 expensive · far · *fast* · hard · never · peace	2 ending · working · looking · loving · *moving* · reaching

1 *fast-moving* ______ : film, traffic, plot
2 ______ : ring, car, apartment
3707 3 ______ : story, problem, speech
4 ______ : nation, politician
5 ______ : person, people
6 ______ : consequences, reforms

8 Sights and sounds of the city (Verbs of perception + object + present participle) ▸ p. 59 • WB (p. 85)

What do you see, hear, etc. when you walk through a city at night? Add a suitable verb and complete the sentences from the notes. Use: **see, listen to, watch**.

1 (people/chat and laugh): You can *hear people chatting and laughing* in street cafés and bars.
2 (people/window-shop): You can ______ in the elegant shopping malls.
3 (crowds/wait): You can ______ at theatres, cinemas and nightclubs.
3708 4 (street musicians/play): You can ______ for waiting crowds.

9 WORDS Word building (Suffixes to make adjectives) ▸ p. 60

a) *Find one adjective for each suffix below:*

-able	-al	-ful	-less	-y
______	______	______	______	______

b) *Katie is in Johannesburg with a group of voluntary workers. Complete part of her e-mail to a friend in the UK. Add the endings in a) to make suitable adjectives from the words in brackets. Remember any necessary prefixes (e. g.* **un-**) *and spelling changes.*

The contrast between rich and poor in Johannesburg is *unbelievable* (not believe). There are rich areas, like Sandton, which is also the ______ (finance) centre, with its banks, ______ (power) global companies, expensive hotels, huge shopping malls. By contrast, the poverty in parts of Soweto is ______ (not imagine). We see poor, ______ (job) people every day, some living in shacks[1] with six children, without water or electricity.

It's ______ (understand) that there's a lot of crime here, but we've been ______ (luck) so far. People working with us on our project are very ______ (help), and the kids watching us are always ______ (cheer) and ______ (fun).

3709 Working here is a sad but ______ (not forget) experience. ☺ We're happy to be here ....

[1] shack [ʃæk] *Hütte*

10 SPEAKING COURSE Part 3: Giving an oral summary ▸ p. 61 • WB (p. 81)

Nina tells a friend about the film 'Blood Diamond'. It is not a good oral summary. First, mark the sentences or sentence parts that you can improve or leave out. Then rewrite the summary in your exercise book and remember to use the present tense. Give an oral summary of the film. You can record your speech.

I saw the film 'Blood Diamond' with my brother last night on TV. It was on quite late, but we had a pizza while we were watching it. It's about the 1999 civil war in Sierra Leone, my brother said.
Well, anyway … erm…, there's lots of fighting between government soldiers and rebels. The pizza was cool, by the way. They force men to work in the diamond mines[1] and take kids from their families and force them to become child soldiers. Well, there's this nice guy, black guy, called Solomon whose family is kidnapped. He's forced to work in the mines and his kid becomes a child soldier, and … well, it's pretty hard stuff. So, Solomon finds this huge diamond. Leo DiCaprio plays Danny Archer, a bad white guy from Zimbabwe who wants the diamond – same as everybody else – but in the end after a lot of confusing stuff he helps the black guy to get back his family in return for the diamond. Oh, and there's this American woman too. She's a kind of journalist. Well, she knows Archer and she publishes the whole story of the dirty diamond deal in her magazine. So this is good, I guess. The film makes you think. My brother liked the fast-moving action, but I don't like cruel stuff. I just close my eyes.

WB, pp. 68–69

11 WORDS Tricky words ▸ p. 62

a) *Match the words that go together. Write lists.*

be … *fun,*

do …

go …

make …

take …

… a break	… a mistake
… business	… notes
… a cake	… on holiday
… an exercise	… on a trip
… for a ride	… photos
… your bed	… a project
… *fun*	… tricks
… homework	… for a walk

b) *Translate the sentences into English. Think carefully how to translate 'machen'.*

1 Ich habe gerade eine englische Übung gemacht. *I've just*

2 Ich habe keine Fehler gemacht. *I haven't*

3 Ich werde jetzt eine kurze Pause machen. *I'm going to*

4 Ich mache mit meinem Freund einen Spaziergang. *I'm going*

3811 5 Englischlernen macht Spaß – nicht wahr? *Learning English*

[1] diamond mine ['daɪəmənd maɪn] *Diamantenmine*

12 Background File: Mumbai ▸ p. 62

a) Tick the correct answer A, B or C. You need the letters in brackets in b).

1 Life expectancy in Mumbai is … in Johannesburg.

A the same as (A) | B longer than (H) | C shorter than (R)

2 In which year did Bombay get its new name 'Mumbai'?

A In 1661. (J) | B In 1947. (O) | C In 1996. (A)

3 For almost 300 years, India was under British control. This is …

A true. (G) | B false. (A) | C not given in the text. (R)

4 Bollywood is …

A Mumbai's financial centre. (P) | B the name of India's film industry. (D) | C a tourist theme park. (U)

5 What is Marathi?

A An Indian language. (N) | B A Mumbai suburb. (U) | C Mumbai's financial centre. (R)

6 Which language is used most for business and in offices?

A Hindi. (G) | B Gujarati. (B) | C English. (I)

b) Now write the letters in brackets from a) in the boxes below. If your answers are correct, the letters make the name of a famous person in India's history.

Here are the question numbers:

3	2	5	4	1	6
___	___	___	___	___	___

INFO BOX

Dharavi, Asia's largest slum area, is in Mumbai. By contrast, the richest people in India also live in Mumbai. The city is the home of more than 20 billionaires!

c) **Extra** *Do research on the person in b). Find out five important facts to present in class.*

13 REVISION If I went to Mumbai, … (Conditional sentences 2) ▸ p. 62

Imagine what you would do and what you wouldn't do if you went to Mumbai. Complete the sentences with **would**, **could** *or* **might**. *You can use ideas from the box or your own ideas.*

- learn about India's history
- take a ride in an auto-rickshaw
- do a Bollywood studios tour
- take an elephant ride
- do voluntary work in the villages
- watch a Bollywood film
- enjoy the delicious food
- take a bus tour of the city
- buy some things at the street markets

1 If I went to Mumbai, *I would/could/might* ____________________

____

2 If I had enough money, I ____________________

____

3 If I had enough time, I ____________________

____

____

3913

14 Arriving in Mumbai (Participle clauses) ▸ p. 66 • WB (pp. 85–86)

Shorten the underlined sentence parts by using a participle clause. Use a present participle or ***having*** *+ past participle.*

1 When I arrived in Mumbai, I was tired after the long flight.

Arriving in Mumbai, I was tired after the long flight.

2 Because I was feeling hot and sticky[1], I was looking forward to a cold shower.

____

3 But when I saw the crowds of people at the taxi stand, I gave up hope of getting to my hotel before midnight.

____

____

4 I stood in the taxi queue and dreamed about a shower and a yummy curry.

____

5 I waited patiently[2] and read my newspaper from the plane.

____

6 When I had arrived at my hotel two hours later, I found that the shower didn't work and the restaurant was closed.

____

____

15 Extra After having a shower, … (Participle clauses with conjunctions) ▸ p. 67 • WB (p. 86)

Where do you need a conjunction to make the meaning clear? Add ***after***, ***although***, ***before*** *or* ***when/while*** *only where necessary.*

1 *After* having a shower, I went down for breakfast.

2 __________ having slept badly, I felt tired.

3 __________ finishing breakfast, I asked the man at reception about city tours.

4 __________ leaving the hotel, I put my passport and most of my money in the room safe.

5 __________ having read about the Mumbai slums, I wasn't surprised by the poverty that I saw.

6 I saw lots of elephants __________ taking a bus tour outside the city.

7 I watched two men __________ repairing an auto rickshaw with a screwdriver[3].

4015 8 I saw a snake __________ having an ice cream in the hotel garden.

[1] sticky ['stɪkɪ] *klebrig* [2] patient ['peɪʃnt] *geduldig* [3] screwdriver ['skruːdraɪvə] *Schraubenzieher*

16 REVISION What would they have done if …? (Conditional sentences 3) ▸ p. 67

Emily and her brother Don were in Mumbai. Rewrite the sentences as conditional sentences (type 3).

1 Emily was too tired, so they didn't do a walking tour of the city.

If Emily hadn't been too tired, they would have done a walking tour of the city.

2 They wanted to take photos of elephants, so they took a bus ride outside the city.

3 Emily felt sick, so they didn't eat bhelpuri at Chowpatty Beach.

4 They wanted to do a Bollywood studios tour, but the tickets were too expensive.

5 They wanted to see the crowded commuter trains, so they went to a train station.

6 They went to Dharavi, so they saw how poor Mumbaikars live.

4116

Now you

*If you **had been** in Mumbai with Don and Emily, which of the things above **would** you **have done**? Write five sentences in your exercise book.*

I think I would have gone to Chowpatty Beach.
I wouldn't have …

17 WRITING An e-mail from Mumbai ▸ p. 68 • WB (pp. 81–82)

Think about what you know about Mumbai from your student's book. Imagine you are there. Write your impressions[1] of the city in an e-mail to an American friend. Write about what you have seen and done, and what you are going to do in the next few days. Use paragraphs and remember your writing skills. Write about 120 words in your exercise book. First, brainstorm your ideas and make notes.

Notes – Mumbai

WB, pp. 63–67

[1] impression [ɪm'preʃn] *Eindruck*

18 MEDIATION Taking care in the sun ▸ p. 68 • WB (p. 79)

a) *Read the questions below first, then scan the text to find the answers. Which questions does the text answer? Tick them (✔). Which questions does the text not answer? Cross them (✘).*

1 Wann sollte man eine Sonnencreme benutzen? ☐

2 Wann sollte man nicht in die Sonne gehen? ☐

3 Was ist beim Schwimmen zu beachten? ☐

4 Wie oft sollte man eine Sonnencreme auftragen? ☐

5 Was ist bei Kindern zu beachten? ☐

6 Wie viel Wasser sollte man in der Sonne trinken? ☐

TAKING CARE IN THE SUN

One of the problems of enjoying the weather in hot countries is not noticing that your body is getting too much sun. When your skin starts to hurt, it's usually too late. However, if you follow a few simple rules, you will get a suntan and not a sunburn.

Sunscreen

Use sunscreen at least half an hour before you go in the sun. This will give it time to work effectively. If the sun is very strong, use an SPF[1] 30. Don't use your old sunscreen from your last year's holiday!

Choose the right time to sunbathe

Plan your sunbathing. Don't go in the sun at the hottest times of day, usually between 11 am and 3 pm. Avoid direct sun. Sit under a tree or umbrella[2] or in the shade of a building. Don't stay in the sun too long. Allow your skin to get used to the sun slowly. Start with ten minutes, then allow yourself five minutes longer in the sun each day.

Sun and water

Wear a T-shirt to protect your back and shoulders when you go in the water. After swimming in the sea, don't sunbathe with saltwater on your skin. If possible, take a shower to wash off the salt. Don't forget to use sunscreen again after your swim.

What to wear in the sun

When you're outdoors but not on a beach, wear long trousers, a cap or hat and sunglasses. Cover your arms and shoulders. Remember that white and light colours are more suitable than black and dark colours.

What to drink

In hot countries your body needs more water than usual. Try to drink at least three litres of water a day. Drink bottled water in countries where the quality of the drinking water may be a problem. Don't drink alcohol in the sun.

b) *Answer the questions in a) for a German friend. Concentrate on the most important points.*

WB, pp. 70–71

[1] SPF = sun protection factor [prəˈtekʃn ˌfæktə] *Sonnenschutzfaktor* [2] umbrella [ʌmˈbrelə] *Schirm*

19 STUDY SKILLS
The Paradox of Mumbai (Summarizing a non-fictional text)

▸ p. 69 • SF (p. 149)

In your exercise book, summarize the following text about Mumbai in your own words. Read the text, make notes on main points and important details, or mark them in different colours. Use the present tense in your summary.

The Paradox of Mumbai

(by Erich Follath, extract from *Slums, Stocks, Stars and the New India*)

Mumbai is at the heart of India's growing economic power. But it is also the place where many of the subcontinent's paradoxes can be found in close quarters. Billionaires, Bollywood stars and slum dwellers[1] all want to be part of the new India.

[...]

Bombay, or Mumbai as it is now officially called, well deserves its nickname, Maximum City [...]
The city is home to India's oldest stock exchange[2], its most important banks, its wealthiest business moguls, its most beautiful movie stars and its most feared gangsters. [...] Forty percent of international flights to India land in this city, which already counts more than 18 million inhabitants today. According to[3] a United Nations estimate[4], it will be the world's second largest city after Tokyo by 2015 – and will have more inhabitants than either Australia or all of Scandinavia.

Bombay is Bollywood, where several hundred films are produced each year, [...] Indeed, the Bombay film industry far outpaces[5] Hollywood when it comes to sheer[6] volume. Rents[7] in the city's most exclusive districts[8] are higher than in Munich, New York or London. World-class restaurants serve up uniquely Indian interpretations of haute cuisine, [...] It is not unheard of for powerful businessmen to arrive for business meetings at the city's top restaurants and hotels driving their Lamborghinis. From their Bombay headquarters, billionaire industrialists [...] become global players as they embark on[9] shopping sprees for attractive takeover[10] targets[11], including major European companies. [...] But Mumbai also holds the dubious[12] distinction[13] of being home to Asia's largest slums where, according to government statistics, 60 percent of all city residents live. In 2003 there were 17 public toilets for every million people, and to this day at least one third of the city's residents have no access[14] to clean drinking water.
The legions of Bombay's poor are growing by the day, as thousands of people migrate from rural areas to the big city, sleeping on its sidewalks and hoping for a better life in this harbor of hope. [...]

(SPIEGEL 9/2007 SPIEGEL ONLINE International/DER SPIEGEL 9/2007)

Now you

Look through Unit 3 of your student's book again and think about the cities of Hong Kong, Johannesburg and Mumbai. Complete these tasks in your exercise book.

a) First, make a list of things you have learned (for example, population, size, historical facts).
b) Make a list of the facts that surprised you the most.
c) In a few sentences describe Britain's historical links with the three cities.
d) Which of the three cities would you choose to visit? Why? Write a paragraph discussing the good and bad aspects of life in your chosen city and giving reasons for your choice[15].

4320
4321

[1] slum dweller [slʌm 'dwelə] *Slumbewohner* [2] stock exchange ['stɒk ɪks,tʃeɪndʒ] *Börse* [3] according to [ə'kɔːdɪŋ tə] *nach, zufolge* [4] estimate ['estɪmət] *Schätzung* [5] outpace [,aʊt'peɪs] *hinter sich lassen* [6] sheer [ʃɪə] *pur* [7] rent [rent] *Miete* [8] district ['dɪstrɪkt] *Gebiet, Bezirk* [9] embark on [ɪm'bɑːk ɒn] *beginnen mit* [10] takeover ['teɪkəʊvə] *Übernahme* [11] target ['tɑːgɪt] *Ziel* [12] dubious ['djuːbiəs] *zweifelhaft* [13] distinction [dɪ'stɪŋkʃn] *Auszeichnung, Unterschied* [14] access ['ækses] *Zugang* [15] choice [tʃɔɪs] *Wahl*

Unit 4 Teen world

1 Typical teens ▸ pp. 78–79

Look at pp. 78–79 of your student's book again. Then answer the questions in note form. Use your notes for a discussion in class.

1 Which aspects of teen life do the photos show?

free time, friendships,

2 Would you say that the photos give a typical picture of teens? Say why you (don't) think so.

Yes, I think the photos are typical, but

3 Think of other important aspects of teen life that the photos do not show.

school, sports,

4 What message does the cartoon on p. 79 of your student's book want to give its readers? Explain.

I think the message of the cartoon is that

2 SPEAKING Teens and their mobiles ▸ p. 81 • WB (pp. 80–81) 14

Listen to what six British students say about how they use their mobile phones. In the pauses, give your opinion on what each student says. Use phrases such as:

- I agree with ... (completely).
- I don't agree with ...
- I can't understand why ...
- I think ... is right/wrong.
- In my opinion, ...
- I don't think it's fair to ...
- It's a good idea to ... because ...
- I think it's stupid to say ... because ...

INFO BOX

In Germany 92 % of young people aged 12 to 19 have a mobile phone, 69 % of kids from 10 to 13, 16 % of kids under 10!
Half of the kids pay part of their monthly mobile bill[1]. 20 % of the kids pay the bill themselves!
(Source: KidsVA 2009, Egmont Ehapa Verlag)

This is how you might give your opinion on what Emma says.

WB, pp. 68–69

1 Emma:
I agree with Emma's parents. In my opinion, Emma is unfair. Why should her parents pay so much money just for her fun? I think that a lot of Emma's phone calls and messages are probably not important anyway. If I was her mum or dad, I wouldn't pay her bills.

4402

[1] bill [bɪl] *Rechnung*

3 STUDY SKILLS Argumentative writing ▸ p. 82 • SF (p. 147)

Write arguments for and against this statement:

Parents should not allow school students to have a TV in their room.

Add arguments and points to the following outline or use your own ideas. Write your complete text in your exercise book or on the computer.

1	Introduction	Almost all school students watch TV in the evening, but should parents allow them to have a TV in their room? ...
2	First point of view	Parents allow their children to have their own TV mostly for practical reasons.
2.1	First argument	First, young people don't always want to see the same programmes as their parents, so they argue. For example, ... teen soap operas ...
2.2	Second argument	...
2.3	...	...
3	Opposite point of view	However, is it really a good idea for school students to watch TV when they want and for as long as they want? ...
3.1	First argument	Young people maybe watch programmes that are bad or not suitable, for example ...
3.2	Second argument	Another argument is that ...
3.3	...	Third, ...
4	Conclusion	After looking at both sides, I think that ...
4.1	Summing up	To sum up, in my opinion ... because there are more disadvantages than advantages for having ...
4.2	Personal opinion	That's why I ...

4 REVISION A date (Talking about the future) ▸ p. 83

Use a future form of the verb in brackets to complete the dialogue: **going to**, **will***-future or present progressive (e. g. is going). Sometimes more than one form is possible.*

1 *Dave* I think I'll go (go) to the match tomorrow.

Steve OK. Great! I ______ (go) with you.

Dave Well, actually ______ (ask) Emma.

Steve Ah. So you ______ (go) on a date!

Dave Not yet. I ______ (meet) her after school to discuss our English project, so I ______ (ask) her then.

Steve Well, good luck!

2 *Emma* I ______ (go) on a date with Dave.

Mel With Dave? Wow! Maybe he ______ (take) you to that new trendy club. What ______ (you, wear)? Your new evening top and your black trousers?

Emma Well, actually I ______ (wear) old jeans and a cap. We ______ (go) to a football match ...

4504

5 EVERYDAY ENGLISH Asking someone out ▸ p. 83

Make a dialogue. Write in your exercise book. The phrases below may help you.

- Well, how about …?
- Have you got any plans for …?
- Shall I pick you up ?
- We could go to …
- It would be so cool if …
- I don't really fancy going …
- I think I'd prefer …
- That would be great. Thanks!

6 WORDS Blue box: German 'schön' usw. ▸ p. 83, p. 191

What is the best translation for German 'schön'? Sometimes more than one word is suitable.

1 Gina is almost 40, but she's still a very *attractive/good-looking* woman.

2 Judith said her Australian surf instructor was seriously ______________ .

3 Film stars don't have to be ______________ – but they usually are.

4 Pat and Rob have two little daughters. They're both very ______________ and intelligent[1] too.

5 We had a ______________ day in the mountains. The scenery was beautiful.

6 Who's the ______________ boy sitting at the corner table?

4606 7 What a ______________ baby!

7 ASBOs ▸ p. 85

a) *Choose words from the box in the correct form to complete the sentences.*

attack • ban • behaviour • cause • court • fights • kick • law • motorbikes offer • order • organization • police • punishment • straighten up • vandalize

1 The 'B' in 'ASBO' means '______________'.

2 The 'O' in 'ASBO' means '______________'.

3 Shane was given a four-year ASBO by the ______________ .

4 He ______________ serious trouble many times.

5 He ______________ footballs against houses and cars.

6 He rode ______________ on the pavement.

7 He ______________ other teenagers.

8 He was ______________ from some areas of town.

9 The ASBO was his ______________ .

10 It helped him to ______________ his life.

b) *Shane is now 17 and doing well. How do you think he feels about himself and about his future? Write a paragraph in your exercise book.*

4607 Ideas: *feels proud of himself • serious about work • looking forward to his future • job and money*

[1] intelligent [ɪn'telɪdʒənt] *intelligent*

8 SPEAKING COURSE Part 4: Talking about ASBOs (Having a discussion)

▸ p. 86 • WB (p. 81) 15, 16

a) Choose and tick the correct phrase. During a discussion, what would you say …

1 … when you want to know someone's opinion?

A I see what you mean. B What do you think?
C Could you say that again, please?

2 … when you say what you think?

A I agree with you. B In my opinion, … C No, that's not right.

3 … when you think/feel the same as the speaker?

A Could you say that again? B I agree with you. C Let me explain.

4 … when you want to say that you understand the speaker's point?

A I see what you mean. B Wait a minute. Let me finish.
C Sorry, I don't agree with you.

5 … when you are speaking and someone else starts to speak?

A No, that's not right. B Could you say that again, please?
C Wait a minute. Let me finish.

6 … when you don't think/feel the same as the speaker?

A Sorry, I don't agree with you. B I know you're right. C That's true.

7 … when you think what someone said is wrong?

A I don't understand what you mean. B You're right. C No, that's not right.

b) Read the discussion phrases below. Then listen to Guy, Mel and Ali (15), three UK teenagers who are talking about ASBOs. Write down the order that you hear the discussion phrases in (1–11).

I agree (with you).	( )	That's a good point.	( )
In my opinion, …	(1)	I see what you mean.	( )
Wait a minute. Let me finish.	( )	Sorry, but I don't agree (with you).	( )
What do you think?	( )	No, that's not right.	( )
First, …	( )	That's true.	( )
Second, …	( )		

c) Listen again to the discussion (16) and in the pauses say the missing phrases. Do this exercise at least twice.

That's a good point. I see what you mean. But I don't agree with you. In my opinion, …

WB, pp. 68–69

4708
4709

9 REVISION Kids causing trouble (Participle clauses) ▸ p. 87 • WB (pp. 85–86)

a) Read part of Jamal's essay. Improve the style by using participle clauses instead of the underlined subordinate clauses. Write the participle clauses.

Young people who get into trouble with the police often have nothing to do. Because they don't have a job to go to, they feel useless and bored. In the area where I live there are often teenagers who hang out in groups on the street or in the shopping mall. Teenagers who cause trouble are not always bad people, but because they want some action in their boring lives, they do wrong things. For example, some kids who spray graffiti are often really good at art.
ASBOs which are given to younger teenagers seem to work well. I know a boy in our area who had an ASBO. As he was not allowed to go out on the streets in the evenings, he started to read books at home. Their TV was broken. He also knew that kids who break their ASBOs can go to prison. He started to work harder in school and he got some GCSEs.
I think that most teenagers who commit crimes need help instead of punishment.

getting into trouble

b) **Extra** *Translate the participle clauses that you have used into German. Write in your exercise book.*

Now you

Do you think that an ASBO is a good way to stop anti-social behaviour? Write a formal letter to a magazine and give reasons for your opinion. Brainstorm your ideas and write notes. Use your exercise book or your computer for your completed letter.

Ideas: ***have nothing to do • no job • no money • feel bored and angry • don't care • need 'fun'***

Dear Sir or Madam
I would like to share my opinion on anti-social behaviour and teenagers with readers of your magazine.
First, ...
Second, ...
Third, ...
...
Yours faithfully

10 Teens who help ▸ pp. 88–89

Test

a) Read pp. 88–89 of your student's book again. Then choose the correct answer, A, B or C.

1 The ManaTEEN club is …

A a diving club. (C) B a volunteer program for teens. (R)
C an environmental group for over 18s. (L)

2 In the Weeki Wachee Springs the divers were looking for …

A turtles. (O) B different kinds of fish. (L) C trash. (A)

3 The Hickory Soup Kitchen is …

A a soup restaurant. (A) B a voluntary[1] organization which gives food to poor people. (O)
C a community kitchen. (S)

4 The Hickory Soup Kitchen …

A cooks soup for the hungry. (F) B collects food only. (R)
C collects food and money for food. (D)

5 Community service in the US is …

A always voluntary. (F) B an important tradition. (L)
C always required by the schools. (D)

6 At Fountain Valley School, community service is …

A required by the school. (F) B required by the parents. (O) C always voluntary. (C)

7 At Fountain Valley School students … do a minimum of ten hours of community service every year.

A are allowed to (S) B have to (I) C should (P)

b) Put the letters after your answers in the right order to give you the name of where the Weeki Wachee Springs can be found: ____________________

4910

11 They make you work hard (let/make somebody do something) ▸ p. 90

a) Underline the correct form in the brackets.

1 Teenagers volunteer to go to boot camp instead of prison. No one (makes/lets) them go.

2 At boot camp they (make/let) you work really hard.

3 They (don't let/don't make) you go home until the six months are over.

4 They (don't make/don't let) you have any contact with family or friends, not even a phone call.

5 The instructors (make/let) you obey stupid orders, just to teach you discipline.

6 The worst thing is, nobody (lets/makes) you think for yourself.

b) What do your parents make you do or not make you do? What do they let you do or not let you do? Write a short text (50–60 words) in your exercise book. You can use these ideas and add your own:

homework • housework • pay your own mobile bill • work for extra money • write thank-you letters • clean your room • help in the kitchen • pay back money that you have borrowed • sleep longer at the weekends • invite your friends whenever you want • stay out late • watch TV until late • have sleepovers

4911

[1] voluntary ['vɒləntrɪ] *freiwillig*

12 What have they had done? (have something done) ▸ p. 90

a) Before and after. What have they had done?

1 hair – dye[1]	2 hair – cut	3 computer – repair
She has *had her hair dyed.*	He has ____	They ____

b) What do you and your family sometimes have done? When or how often? Write sentences.

1 car/wash: *My dad never has our car washed. He washes it himself.*

2 hair/cut ____

3 pizza/deliver: ____

5012 4 eyes/test: ____

13 MEDIATION International work camps ▸ p. 91 • WB (p. 79)

Tell a British exchange student the main facts from the following website information: who takes part in the work camp programmes, how long you stay, what kind of work you do, how long you work, free-time activities, etc. Make notes in English in your exercise book first. Prepare a two-minute talk to present in class.

Internationale *work camps* für Teenager

Wer, wo und wann?
Jedes Jahr nehmen junge Leute aus aller Welt an Hilfsprojekten in internationalen *work camps* in über hundert Ländern teil. Dabei lernen die Teilnehmer/innen nicht nur andere Länder und Kulturen kennen. Bei einem Aufenthalt von zwei bis sechs Wochen arbeiten sie zusammen an einem sinnvollen Projekt. Die Camps finden meist in den Monaten Juni bis September für die Altersgruppen von 14 bis 19 Jahren statt.

Arbeitsgruppen und Arbeitsbereiche
In jeder *Work-camp*-Gruppe sind 10 bis höchstens 20 Teilnehmer/innen, die jeden Tag ca. vier Stunden mit einem/einer Gruppenleiter/in zusammenarbeiten. Die Arbeitsbereiche sind vielfältig, z.B. Umweltprojekte, die Betreuung von Kindern, Englischunterricht, Mitarbeit in Krankenhäusern oder Waisenhäusern, die Renovierung von Schulen, Jugendzentren und Spielplätzen oder historischen Gebäuden. Die Campsprache ist meist Englisch.

Unterbringung und Freizeit
Unterkünfte, z.B. in Jugendzentren oder Jugendherbergen werden zur Verfügung gestellt. Auch die Verpflegung ist kostenfrei. Oft wird nicht nur zusammen gegessen, sondern unter Anleitung auch zusammen gekocht. Freizeitaktivitäten kommen auch nicht zu kurz. Zum Freizeitprogramm gehören nicht nur gemeinsame Ausflüge und Sightseeing, sondern auch Workshops. Viel Sport sowie Fahrradtouren und Wanderungen gehören auch dazu.

WB, pp. 70–71

[1] dye [daɪ] *färben*

14 WRITING International work camps ▸ p. 91 • WB (pp. 81–82)

Test

WB, pp. 63–67

What do you think about volunteering for work abroad? Think of arguments for and against working at an international work camp. List advantages and disadvantages. Write about 150 words in your exercise book. Remember to use paragraphs, topic sentences and your writing skills.

Young people often decide to volunteer for work after school, before they start university or in the summer holidays ...

15 My book quiz ▸ p. 91

How well do you know your student's book? Test yourself! Write short answers.

1. The capital of Australia is ______
2. The name of the famous rock that is important to the Aboriginal culture is ______
3. Name three animals which are unique to Australia: ______
4. The kind of football that Australians play is called ______
5. The paper that tells others about your education and work experience is called your ______
6. In the USA your 'CV' is called your ______
7. When you apply for a job, you must also send a letter of ______
8. Which city has the biggest population: Mumbai, Johannesburg or Hong Kong? ______
9. Soweto is a famous township of which city? ______
10. What is the name of India's film industry? ______
11. Who became South Africa's first black president? ______
12. About how many people live in Berlin? ______
13. In what year did India become independent from Britain? ______
14. UK courts don't always send young troublemakers to prison. They give them ______
15. In the US troublemakers can choose to go to ______ instead of prison.

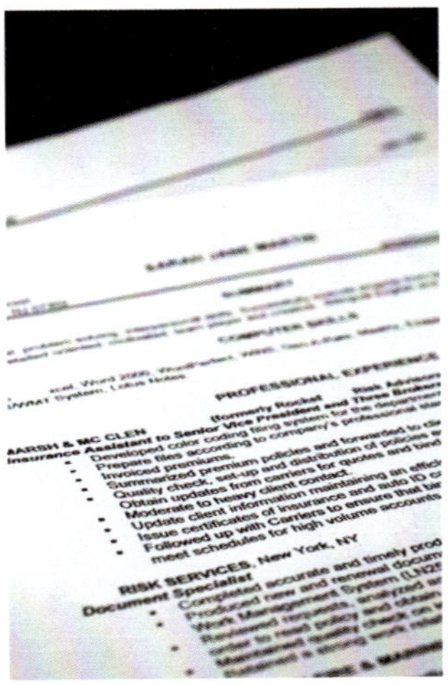

16 READING WORKING WITH THE TEXT The caller ▸ pp. 92–95 • WB (pp. 77–78)

a) *How well do you know the story? Read the summary carefully. Some details are not correct. Mark wrong sentences, sentence parts or words.*

Lindsay's Aunt Margaret has died. After the funeral Lindsay's dad can't find his cellphone. Later at home, when Lindsay gets a call from a voice that says it's Aunt Margaret, she thinks it's her friend Candice who is playing a trick on her. Lindsay goes to Missy's party and wears Aunt Margaret's diamond earrings to make the other girls jealous. When the voice of Aunt Margaret calls Lindsay again on her father's cellphone, Lindsay thinks it's her brothers who are playing a trick. Lindsay tells the voice that she was only nice to her because she wanted her earrings. That evening all the girls stay at Missy's house. Lindsay gets a third call from the unknown caller on her father's cellphone. The voice says she's coming back to get the earrings. Lindsay thinks it's her brothers again who have found the phone and are trying to scare her. Lindsay calls home, but her mom says the boys are playing cards. In the middle of the call the lights go out at Lindsay's house and there's a loud noise. Then someone knocks at the back door of Missy's house. Lindsay is scared. She wants Missy to see who is at the door. Missy leaves Lindsay alone upstairs. Then Missy's phone rings again. Lindsay hears a knock on the window and is afraid that it's Aunt Margaret's ghost. The voice behind the bedroom door sounds like Missy's, laughing at Lindsay because she's crying like a baby. Angry with Missy, Lindsay opens the door, but it is not Missy who is holding the phone in a muddy hand …

b) *Some things happen in the story that can't be explained in a logical way. Find examples of this in the text and summarize them in your own words.*

Lindsay's father loses his cellphone after the funeral.

c) *Could there be a logical explanation for the events of the story 'The caller'? For example, is someone perhaps playing Lindsay a trick to scare her and teach her a lesson[1]? Write your thoughts.*

WB, pp. 58–62

d) *What makes a good scary story? Think about a scary film you have seen or a scary book you have read. Write notes in your exercise book and discuss your ideas in class.*

5217
5218

a strange person or strange people, a lonely place, …

[1] teach sb. a lesson *jm. eine Lektion erteilen*

How well can you do these things?

	Very well	OK	Practise!
LISTENING AND READING SKILLS: I can …			
… follow a class presentation, e.g. about a big city.	☐	☐	☐
… read longer fictional and non-fictional texts without difficulty, e.g. *The caller* (SB pp. 92–94).	☐	☐	☐
… understand the difference between a subjective and an objective report. An objective report gives only facts, not opinions or feelings.	☐	☐	☐
SPEAKING AND WRITING SKILLS: I can …			
… give an oral summary of a film or TV programme using only information about the events, not personal opinion.	☐	☐	☐
… summarize the main points of a non-fictional text. First I make notes from the original.	☐	☐	☐
… write an argumentative text, giving arguments and examples for and against a statement, then summing up the main points with my personal opinion, e.g. on the use of mobiles at school.	☐	☐	☐
MEDIATION SKILLS: I can …			
… summarize and report the main facts of a conversation or written text from German into English or from English into German.	☐	☐	☐
… use my own words in my summary. I do not translate the original conversation or written text.	☐	☐	☐
TOPICS: I have learned …			
… about the problems of big cities, e.g. pollution, crime, waste disposal, clean water, traffic noise, poverty.	☐	☐	☐
… about teenage activities, interests and hobbies, e.g. mobile behaviour, relationships, volunteer work and community service.	☐	☐	☐
… problems of teenagers who behave anti-socially and punishments for anti-social behaviour, e.g. ASBOs in the UK, boot camps in the USA.	☐	☐	☐
STUDY AND LANGUAGE SKILLS: I know …			
… how to use an English grammar to improve expression.	☐	☐	☐
… how to use an English-English dictionary.	☐	☐	☐
… how an author can create suspense in literary texts.	☐	☐	☐

HOW I COULD IMPROVE MY ENGLISH SKILLS: I could …

(e.g. work through parts of Skills Check 2 again, read the Skills file in my SB in detail …)

____

____

____

____

____

LISTENING

In this part of your workbook you will find exercises that will help you with your skills: listening, reading, writing, speaking, mediation.

1 School chat (Listening for gist) ▸ *WB (p. 77)* 17

Listen to four short dialogues. What are the friends talking about? Match the letters A–D to the correct topic.

A	A project
B	A school trip
C	Weekend plans
D	The school team

Tip 1

Think about the four topics. Which **words/word fields** might you expect to hear? Listen for those words.
For example:
project > *research, subject, finish*
school trip > *bus/train, place, time*
weekend plans > *friends, party*
school team > *match, game, play*

2 The Olympic Games (Listening for gist) ▸ *WB (p. 77)* 18

Read statements A–E. Then listen to four students talking about the Olympic Games. Match the correct statement to each student. There is one statement that you do not need.

A I'm a sporty person, so I love the summer Olympics.

B I think the Olympic Games have become too political.

C The Games have become too spectacular and too expensive.

D I'm not into sport, so I don't really follow the Games on TV.

E It's great that Olympic athletes are so disciplined and work so hard. We can all learn from such people.

5402 Student 1: ☐ Student 2: ☐ Student 3: ☐ Student 4: ☐

Tip 2

Before you listen, concentrate[1] on the statements.
Decide which are **positive** and which are **negative**.
When you listen, notice how the speakers give their opinion. Is their tone of voice positive or negative?

3 Tricky numbers, times, letters (Listening for detail) ▸ *WB (p. 77)* 19

Listen and mark what you hear: one of each pair.

a) Numbers: 245 / 254 | 14 / 40 | 98 / 89 | 60 / 16 | 02256691 / 02256651 | 1978 / 1987

b) Times: 2.30 / 2.13 | 12.30 / 1.30 | 4.30 / 3.30 | 9.15 / 9.50

5403 *c)* Letters: A / E | E / I | A / R | G / J | J / G

Tip 3

When you listen the first time, write down **names, places, dates, numbers, times** or **letters** exactly. They are easily confused.
For example: *30* or *13*? *7E* or *7A*?
When you listen a second time, check your notes and concentrate on the answers you still need.

4 At the station (Listening for detail) ▸ *WB (p. 77)* 20

You are going to hear three short train announcements. First read the statements below carefully. Then listen to the announcements and decide whether the statements are true or false. Tick a box.

		True	False
1	The train to Edinburgh will leave from platform 6.	☐	☐
2	Departure will be delayed by 13 minutes.	☐	☐
3	The 12.15 train to Bristol will not leave from platform 9 today.	☐	☐
4	The Bristol train will now leave from platform 7E.	☐	☐
5	The train from York will now arrive at platform 3 at 12.43.	☐	☐

5404

[1] concentrate ['kɒnsntreɪt] *konzentrieren*

5 The London Eye (Listening for detail) ▸ WB (p. 77) 21

Listen to a guide telling tourists about the London Eye. Then choose the correct answer, A, B or C.

1 The tourists' ride on the Eye is booked[1] for ...

A 2.30 pm. B 3.30 pm. C 4.30 pm.

2 How far can you see on a clear day?

A 40 miles. B 40 kilometres. C 14 kilometres.

3 When did work on the London Eye start?

A 1990. B 1991. C 1992.

4 How many passenger capsules[2] are there?

A 23. B 25. C 32.

5 The London Eye is now the ... biggest wheel in the world.

5505

A second B third C fourth

Tip 4

Often information is given **indirectly**, in different words. For example:
'When did work on the Eye start?'
You hear only:
'It took *7* years to build and it was opened in *1999*.' But you can work out the answer from this information.

6 BE and AE (BE and AE pronunciation) ▸ WB (p. 77) 22–24

a) *Listen to the words (22). Is the pronunciation BE or AE? Write **A** (American) or **B** (British).*

1		5		9	
2		6		10	
3		7		11	
4		8		12	

5506

Tip 5

	BE	AE
grass, can't	[ɑː]	[æ]
knew, Tuesday	[juː]	[uː]
not, got	[ɒ]	[ɑ]
first, world, more	> in AE you hear the 'r'	
little, city, writer	> in AE 't' in the middle of a word sounds like 'd'	

b) *Now look carefully at the sentences below. Mark the sounds which are pronounced differently in AE. Then listen (23) and check that you have marked all the differences. You'll hear each sentence twice: first in BE then in AE.*

1 It's so hot in here! Let's go to the park! I'll ask my sister if she wants to join us.

2 Let's have a nice cool drink first. How about a glass of mineral water? Or some coffee?

3 I forgot to tell you. We have a new student in our class. It's her birthday soon. She's invited us all to a party.

c) *You are in a tourist information office in London. Listen (24) to what people are asking. Are they British or American? Write the numbers of the speakers under the right flag.*

Speakers ______________________

Speakers *1,* ______________________

[1] book [bʊk] *buchen, reservieren* [2] capsule ['kæpsjuːl] *Kapsel*

7 At the youth hostel (Accents) ▸ WB (p. 77) 25

You hear some young people talking about why tourists like to visit their countries. Do they come from the UK, the USA or Australia? Write the country under the photo.

5607 1 ____________ 2 ____________ 3 ____________ 4 ____________ 5 ____________ 6 ____________

8 Problems (Fast speech) ▸ WB (p. 77) 26, 27

Listen (26) to three teenagers talking about their problems. They talk at a normal speed, but in everyday speech some words are shortened or missed out. Listen for the forms in Tip 6 too. Who says what? Write the names in 1–4 below: Todd, Will or Liz.

1 ____________ and ____________ are having problems with parents.

2 ____________ 's parents are not so strict with his younger brother.

3 ____________ doesn't know how to solve his problem with his girlfriend.

4 ____________ is having problems at school with her grades.

Tip 6

When people talk quickly, they may use expressions that are not grammatically correct. You hear the following forms especially in AE. Maybe you've heard these forms in song lyrics too:

gonna	>	'going to'
wanna	>	'want to'
gotta	>	'have got to'
kinda	>	'kind of'
dunno	>	'don't know'

b) *Listen (27) to the rest of the conversation. This time the friends talk faster. Listen carefully for short or ungrammatical forms. Then tick true or false.*

	True	False
1 Liz doesn't want to give up her weekend job.	☐	☐
2 Liz thinks she'll talk to her Math teacher and her Science teacher.	☐	☐
3 Will's girlfriend is called Katie.	☐	☐
4 Will doesn't always work on Friday evenings.	☐	☐
5 Will has a job at a pizza place.	☐	☐
6 Will has a friend called Matt.	☐	☐
7 Will's girlfriend went to a movie with a boy called Stevie.	☐	☐
8 Todd says Will has to trust[1] his girlfriend more.	☐	☐

[1] trust [trʌst] *(ver)trauen*

9 Talking about jobs (Listening skills) ▸ WB (p. 77) 28

a) Listen to five young people talking about jobs. First, read the statements below and the list of names. Then listen to what they say. Choose the correct statement below for each person. Write A–E next to the names.

A 'I've found a job as a waitress[1] in a café, but I won't find out details until I call again later today.'

B 'I had a big problem on my first day. The manager wasn't very happy.'

C 'I've applied for some jobs I got from the job centre. I've had just one job offer so far.'

D 'I enjoy my work now, but at first I wasn't allowed to serve[2] customers[3] because I had to learn the job.'

E 'I wanted to work with computers, but I'm learning to repair cars now. I like it.'

1 Dylan: ☐ *2* Sophie: ☐ *3* Gina: ☐

4 Jamie: ☐ *5* Leo: ☐

b) Now listen again, this time for detail. Choose the correct answer and tick the box.

1 Dylan is looking for …

☐ a summer job. ☐ a job after school. ☐ a Saturday job.

2 Dylan found some jobs at the job centre, and he has applied for …

☐ four. ☐ five. ☐ six.

3 Sophie already has some job experience …

☐ in a hotel. ☐ in a café. ☐ in a restaurant.

4 Sophie has to call again about the job at …

☐ 1.30. ☐ 2.30. ☐ 3.30.

5 Gina is from …

☐ Australia. ☐ the UK. ☐ the USA.

6 Gina works in a flower shop …

☐ from nine to five. ☐ from nine to six. ☐ after school.

7 Jamie has a …

☐ part-time job. ☐ holiday job. ☐ full-time job.

8 Jamie works in …

☐ Glasgow. ☐ Aberdeeen. ☐ a village near Aberdeen.

9 Leo has been working in a travel agency …

☐ for a week. ☐ for a month. ☐ since he left school.

10 Leo sent the wrong flight tickets to Mrs White. She wanted to go to …

☐ Johannesburg. ☐ Hawaii. ☐ Alaska.

[1] waitress ['weɪtrəs] *Kellnerin* [2] serve [sɜːv] *bedienen* [3] customer ['kʌstəmə] *Kunde/-in*

READING

10 ESL in L.A. (1) (Skimming) ▸ *WB (p. 78)*

*You would like to visit Los Angeles and maybe do an English course. You find this information on the internet. Would it be useful to you? Who is the information for? **Skim** the text for a few seconds. Then tick A, B or C.*

The information is for …

A teachers of ESL.

B American college students.

C foreign[1] students of English.

ESL in L.A.	
ESL programs	Our programs cover all areas of English as a second language. We offer intensive programs and exam preparation programs for college and university entrance.
Course levels	We offer courses for **beginners**, **intermediate** and **advanced** levels[2]. All levels offer training in reading, listening, speaking and writing skills, vocabulary building, pronunciation and grammar. Courses in **American culture**, English for **business and commerce**, English for **science and technology** are offered at intermediate and advanced levels only.
Course hours	9 am–12 am, 2 pm–5 pm or 6 pm–9 pm, Mon–Fri. There are no weekend courses.
Course groups	**Intensive programs**: groups of 6–8 students. All other course groups: 12–15 students.
Teaching staff	All our teachers are college and university trained professionals and are **native speakers**.
Location	Centrally located close to city attractions, shopping and eating within walking distance.
Accommodation	Students may choose to stay with a selected **host family** or at a **residence club** (single room, with breakfast and dinner).

5810

Tip 7

Step *1*: Look at the **form** of the text. Is it a newspaper article, a fictional text, an information brochure?

Step *2*: Look at the **title**, **headings** and **pictures**.

Step *3*: Look at the words in **bold** type.

11 ESL in L.A. (2) (Scanning) ▸ *WB (p. 78)*

*Now scan the text in exercise 10 to find the answers to these questions. The key words are in **bold** for you. Write notes.*

1 What does '**ESL**' mean? __________

2 How many **course levels** are offered? __________

3 Do all courses teach **American culture**? __________

4 **Where** is the school? __________

5 Are there any courses at the **weekend**? __________

6 How many students are there in the **intensive** program groups? __________

7 How many kinds of **accommodation** does the school help with? __________

5811 8 Which meals are given with the **accommodation**? __________

Tip 8

Concentrate only on the **key words** in the questions when you scan. Read **around** a key word to find the answers. Remember, you may find a key word in different places in the text, not just in one.

[1] foreign ['fɒrɪn] *ausländisch* [2] advanced level [əd'vɑːnsd] *fortgeschrittenes Niveau*

12 Getting into London (Marking key words; taking notes) ▸ WB (p. 78)

a) *You need information about different kinds of transport into London from Heathrow Airport. Choose and mark key words for the most important information.*

Getting into London from Heathrow

From Heathrow Airport you can take a train, the tube, a coach or a taxi into London.

1 If you want to go by train, the Heathrow Express takes you to Paddington Station in just 15–20 minutes. Trains run every 15 minutes. Cost: £16.50.

2 By tube the journey takes 45 minutes. Heathrow is on the Piccadilly line. There are three tube stations at the airport serving[1] different terminals. The tube stops at famous places in the capital such as Hyde Park Corner, Piccadilly Circus and Covent Garden. Tube trains leave every five minutes. Cost: £4.50.

3 You can take the National Express coach from the Central Bus Station (near Terminals 1, 2 and 3) to Victoria Coach Station in central London. The journey by coach takes 45–75 minutes. There are three to six buses an hour. Cost: £5.

4 By taxi the journey takes 30–75 minutes. Cost for up to five passengers: £40–70.

(Prices: 26.02.2010)

b) *A friend asks you what you have found out. Use your key words to make short notes to tell your friend.*

1 train: Heathrow Express>Paddington, 15–20 min, every 15 min., £16.50

2 __________

3 __________

4 __________

13 Florida's Marine Park (Reading for detail) ▸ WB (p. 78)

Before you read the text about Marine Park, read the statements on the next page. Mark key words in the statements. Look for the answers and tick true, false or not given.

Tip 9

If there are no or not many words in **bold** in the text, choose your own key words from the questions. Look for them when you scan the text and read **around** them.

Opening times

Marine Park is open to visitors every day from 9 am to 7 pm, and from 9 am to 9 pm in the summer months and at holiday times.

How to get here

If you are driving, you will find us just 10 miles northwest of downtown Tampa. From Tampa International Airport it's just a 20-minute taxi ride. Our main entrance and car park for 3,500 vehicles are on South Marine Drive. You can't miss us! Please visit our website for detailed directions.

Admission

1-Day tickets: adults $83.95 (plus tax[2]), children (3–10) years $69.95 (plus tax). Children two years and under go free. There are discounts for senior citizens. Please show your ID.

Online tickets: For tickets bought online 7 days in advance, there is a standard price of $69.95 (plus tax). You can print your ticket at home and there's no waiting at the park entrance.

Florida visitors: Please see our special online offers for 1-day and 3-day tickets.

Florida residents[3]: Please see our special annual and vacation offers.

5913

[1] serve [sɜːv] *bedienen* [2] tax [tæks] *Steuer* [3] resident [rezɪdənt] *Bewohner*

	True	False	Not given
1 The park is open all year round from 9 am to 9 pm.	☐	☐	☐
2 Marine Park is 10 miles northwest of Tampa.	☐	☐	☐
3 It's a 30-minute drive from Tampa International Airport.	☐	☐	☐
4 You enter Marine Park from South Marine Drive.	☐	☐	☐
5 Adult tickets are cheaper online.	☐	☐	☐
6 There is no US tax on tickets.	☐	☐	☐
7 You can use online tickets for one year.	☐	☐	☐
8 There are special ticket offers for Florida residents.	☐	☐	☐
9 You can buy Quick Queue tickets.	☐	☐	☐
10 Children under three years of age are free.	☐	☐	☐

14 Marine Park visitor information (Reading for detail) ▸ *WB (p. 78)*

Read the visitor information sign carefully. It is not important to understand all the words when you read the first time. Complete the sentences below with words from the text.

Marine Park Visitor Information

Please note that before you enter the park, all bags will be examined by our security staff. It is not permitted[1] to bring sharp[2] or dangerous objects into the park, including pocket knives, cans and glass bottles. Please leave these objects in your vehicle.

Visitors are asked not to bring food and drinks into the park. Restaurants and stands selling snacks and soft drinks can be found in several park areas. Exception: baby food and food for special diets.

Visitors are reminded that all indoor areas of the park are smoke-free. Outdoor smoking areas are clearly marked on your park map. If you wish to smoke, please do so in these areas only.

Information about animal feeding times can be found in the park map. Please do not try to feed the animals. It's bad for the animals and may be dangerous for you.

If you wish to bring along your pets, they can wait for you in our air-conditioned pets' area near the main entrance. Please walk your dog at regular intervals during your park visit and bring along enough pet food for the length of your stay. Our pet service costs just $12 a day.

Please note: For safety reasons, visitors are not allowed to bring objects into the park which are ______________ or __________________ . You can buy soft drinks and snacks in the park, so you are asked not to bring your own _______________________ . _______________ is only permitted in some areas.

Please follow the signs. Details of ____________________________ can be found in the _________________ .

There's also a service that looks after visitors' ____________ , so you can bring along your dog or cat too – for just $12 a day.

Tip 10

The words in the task are often different from the words in the text. But the meaning is the same.
Try to work out the meaning of the unknown words from the context.

[1] permit [pəˈmɪt] *gestatten* [2] sharp [ʃɑːp] *scharf*

15 What does it mean? (Working out the meaning of words) ▸ WB (p. 77)

Look at the text in exercise 14 again. How did you work out the meaning of words that are new? Write the words below in the lists with their German meaning. Some words fit in two lists. Decide what helped you most.

exception • examined • staff • length • vehicle • stand • diet • air-conditioned • entrance • intervals

... from the context	... like a German word	... from a part of the word or from the word family
staff – Personal		

6115

16 Saving our planet (Reading skills) ▸ WB (pp. 77–78)

This is part of a text about the earth's problems. Read it carefully. It is not important to understand all the words the first time you read.

Saving our planet

1 Climate change is thought by scientists to be a major problem. In less than a hundred years from now, the earth's average temperature could have risen by as much as five degrees. People living in cold countries may like the idea, but the temperature rise would put the earth and its peoples in danger, as a warmer climate would have disastrous effects on the future of man and nature.

2 A main cause is that humans produce 'greenhouse gases', for example, when burning oil, gas or wood for energy. Industries are a major cause of this. CO2 is released into the atmosphere. This leads to the 'greenhouse effect', as the sun's heat is trapped by too many greenhouse gases in the atmosphere, so the earth gets warmer. Deforestation is another cause, as forests and rainforests absorb carbon dioxide.

3 The effects of global warming could be catastrophic. The ice at the poles could melt, so sea levels would rise – maybe by up to two metres in the next 150 years, some experts believe. This would mean that cities like New York, London or Tokyo might slowly disappear under the sea. Millions of people could be permanently homeless. Some countries could become seriously overpopulated. There may be more natural disasters, like tsunamis and tornadoes. Tropical diseases would spread more quickly into non-tropical countries. The heat could damage the food we grow. Food prices would rise and millions could become hungry. There might not be enough drinking water, so wars might start. Some animals and plants might die out because they could not survive in saltwater.

4 In order to slow down climate change, we must reduce global warming, for example, by using less energy in our daily lives. We should stop burning oil and gas, which produce carbon dioxide and are non-renewable. We should use more renewable energy like solar or wind power. We should save electricity and water, and produce less waste by recycling. We could buy recyclable and energy-efficient products (light bulbs, fridges, computers, etc.). We could plant more trees. We must stop cutting down rainforests. All this and much more ...

***a)** Choose a heading for each paragraph. Write A–D after the numbers.*

1 ☐ 2 ☐

3 ☐ 4 ☐

A Solutions[1]

B Problems

C Consequences

D Reasons

***b)** Look at the text again. How can you work out the meaning of words that are new? Write the words in the lists 1–3 below with their German meaning. Some words fit in two lists. Decide what helped you most.*

release · absorb · greenhouse gas · poles · melt · disaster · deforestation · overpopulation · tropical · major · renewable · recyclable · energy-efficient · rainforest

1 I can understand these words from the **context**: ____________________

____

2 These words are like **German** words: ____________________

____

3 I know **part** of these words or a word from the **word family**: ____________________

____

***c)** Read the statements carefully. Is the information true, false or not in the text? Tick a box.*

	True	False	Not in the text
1 At the end of this century the earth's temperature could be a few degrees warmer.	☐	☐	☐
2 Households produce about a third of carbon dioxide.	☐	☐	☐
3 Carbon dioxide is a 'greenhouse gas'.	☐	☐	☐
4 Natural gas is a renewable source of energy.	☐	☐	☐
5 A lot of the waste that we produce every day finds its way into the seas and oceans.	☐	☐	☐
6 Recyclable products help to reduce waste.	☐	☐	☐
7 Rainforests are burned down so that cattle farmers can produce more meat for export.	☐	☐	☐
8 CO2 cannot be absorbed.	☐	☐	☐

***d)** Now complete these sentences with information from the text.*

1 Climate change is thought to be a major problem because ____________________

____

2 We all produce 'greenhouse gases' by ____________________

3 The earth is getting warmer because ____________________

4 If the ice at the poles melted, ____________________. As a result ____________________

____

5 Maybe people would not have enough to eat because the ____________________

6 Wars might break out because ____________________

[1] solution [sə'lu:ʃn] *Lösung*

WRITING

17 Collecting ideas (Brainstorming) ▸ WB (p. 80)

a) *Choose three topics from A–F below. Brainstorm ideas that you could use in an e-mail to a friend. Make a list or a mind map for each of your three topics in your exercise book.*

A	My free-time activities	D	Work experience
B	My favourite magazine	E	My best birthday
C	My ideal job	F	Raising money for charities

Tip 11

Remember to cross out ideas you won't use and number the useful ideas.

My free-time activities
2 sports
football training
~~skateboarding~~
basketball team
1 friends
shopping
texting
parties
hanging out
3 homework

b) *Use your notes from a) to write an e-mail to an English-speaking friend about one of your topics. Write 80–100 words in your exercise book.*

Hi ...!
Thanks for your last mail. You wanted to know about what I do in my free time. Well, I expect I do the same as you – I often spend time with my friends. Sometimes we go to the local shopping mall and look at CDs and DVDs ...

18 Giving information (The 5 Ws) ▸ WB (p. 80)

a) *A good text gives the reader important information about* **who**, **what**, **where**, **when** *and* **why**. *The text below reports a street accident. In what order does it answer the 5 Ws?*

Tip 12

The **5 Ws** are important, both in reading and writing.
In a good story/report, etc, you find answers to most of the **5** Ws in the first two or three sentences. *Why... ?* and *How...?* sometimes come later.
The **order** of the information is not important and can be different from text to text.

Teenager hit by cyclist[1]

At 10.30 last night a 15-year-old girl was hurt by a cyclist as she was crossing Radfield Road on her way home after visiting a friend. The cyclist, who admitted[2] that he was riding fast on the empty road, ran into the girl, who was wearing dark clothes. The cyclist said, 'She came from nowhere. I just didn't see her.' The cyclist called an ambulance and the girl was treated for a broken finger and shock.

1 *When? – at 10.30 last night*

2 ______

3 ______

4 ______

5 ______

6318

b) *Now write a short text about your last school trip, or your last holiday. Give information about the 5 Ws in the first few sentences, as in the text in a). Write 80–100 words in your exercise book.*

Last year in ... our class went on a trip to .... with ...../Our last class trip took place in ... this year ...

[1] cyclist ['saɪklɪst] *Radfahrer/in* [2] admit [əd'mɪt] *zugeben*

19 Making changes ▸ WB (pp. 81–82)

Tip 13

You can:
- change active to passive or passive to active.
- add a subordinate clause.
- change direct to indirect speech.
- make one sentence out of two using a linking word.
- change the linking word, e.g. *so > because*, *but > although*.

a) Here are some tips that will help you when you want to write a text. Read **Tip 13** *and study the following sentences carefully.*

1 After three days the police caught the escaped prisoner. They had been told where they could find him.
Change active to passive and passive to active.
The escaped prisoner was caught after a few days. Someone had told the police where to find him.

2 It was a cold day in winter when Leila packed her bags and left home to start a new life in Pakistan. She had never met the man she was going to marry.
Add a relative clause – *where …*, and make one sentence out of two.
On a cold winter day Leila left home for Pakistan, where she would start a new life with a husband she had never met.

3 'I'll never be able to wear jeans and tops again, no trainers either,' Leila thought sadly.
Change direct to indirect speech; use group words, not details – *western clothes for jeans, tops, trainers.*
Leila was sad that she would never be able to wear western clothes again.

4 After breakfast, Rob and Pete started their bike tour. The sun was shining. There was a warm breeze and only a few white clouds in the sky.
Make one sentence out of two with a linking word, here: *When …*; leave out details of weather description.
When Rob and Pete started their cycle tour in the morning, the weather was very good.

5 Tom always needs money, so he does a newspaper round before school and he sometimes works in his cousin's café on Wilmore Street after school. He washes cars and does garden work for the neighbours.
Change the linking word – *so > because.* Leave out job details.
Because Tom always needs money, he does lots of jobs before and after school.

b) Now rewrite the following sentences and shorten them where possible. Make one sentence. Remember to use what you have read in a) above.

1 It was really cold in the house, so Polly made a big pot of hot tea for everybody.

Polly made ______________________________

2 US border police send back hundreds of illegal Mexican immigrants every month. Pedro was one of them.

Pedro was ______________________________

3 Jerry arrived late at the airport because of the traffic on the motorway. He found that his plane to Vancouver had already left.

When Jerry ______________________________

4 'There's so much to prepare before the visitors arrive – the flat to clean, shopping to do, food to cook,' thought Emily nervously.

Emily was nervous ______________________________

5 The climbers knew that they would be in serious difficulties if the weather didn't improve.

____

c) Now summarize the following paragraphs taken from different text types. There are many possible ways to do this, but your text should have the main facts and be much shorter.

1 From an article in a local newspaper:

Local boy 19-year-old Josh Turner has come back from a trip of a lifetime. He spent September and October doing volunteer work on a sheep station in New South Wales, Australia. Josh said he wanted to do something really different – and he did. He enjoyed the new experience so much that he would like to go again next year ...

2 From an accident report:

A 50-year-old man and his wife are in a critical condition[1] after their Toyota crashed into a Mercedes truck on the M4 motorway near Bracknell yesterday evening at about 10 o'clock. Roads were wet after heavy[2] rain and there were areas of thick fog. The injured couple were taken to hospital. The driver of the truck was unhurt. When questioned by the police, he said that he had suddenly seen the Toyota coming towards him on the wrong side of the road. He had tried to ...

3 From a novel:

Sarah had never seen such an amazing sight before. Her heart beat loudly with excitement as she walked to the edge[3] of the canyon and looked down at the Colorado River more than one kilometre below. She couldn't believe how lucky she was to be able to visit this natural wonder ...

20 An informal letter (Structuring a text) ► *SF (p. 146)*

Write to a friend about an interesting time that you remember well, for example a day trip, a birthday celebration, a camping trip, a visit to somewhere exciting, etc. Brainstorm your ideas first. Remember to start with the 5 Ws and to use paragraphs. Here are a few ideas. Write about 100 words in your exercise book.

Hi/Hello...!/Dear ...
Thanks for your mail. You must have had a great time last weekend.
Did I tell you about ...?
... is a fantastic place. There's so much ... including ... We had a lot of fun.
First we ... after that we ... , In the evening ...
I have to stop now because ...
Love, /Best wishes,

Tip 14

Give your text:
- a **beginning**. Say what you are going to write about. Start with an interesting opening sentence.
- a **middle**. Give details of events, etc. with a new paragraph for each new idea, starting with a general topic sentence.
- an interesting **end** and a personal closing sentence.

[1] condition [kən'dɪʃn] *Zustand* [2] heavy [hevɪ] *stark, schwer* [3] edge [edʒ] *Kante*

21 Writing a formal letter ▸ SF (p. 146)

a) *Complete the text with words and phrases that are correct for formal letters.*

You put your own address ___at the top on the right___, but you don't write your name. Under your address you write ___the date___. The address of the person you are writing to is written ___on the left___.
You begin a formal letter with '___Dear Sir or Madam___' when you don't know the name of the person you are writing to. Remember that the first word of the first paragraph starts with a ___big (letter)___ letter – which is different from German. You shouldn't use ___short___ forms in formal letters. Write 'I am' and 'I would' instead of 'I'm' and 'I'd'.
You finish a formal letter with '___Yours faithfully___' if you don't know the name of the person you are writing to. If you know the name, you start with '___Dear Mr./Ms.___' and you finish with '___Sincerely___'.

b) *Lina Schneider from Munich writes a letter of application for a job as assistant receptionist[1] at a hotel in London for six weeks in the summer. What belongs where in a formal letter? Choose the correct parts from the list on the right and write the number in the correct place in the letter below.*

8

4

9

5

7

6

2

Lina Schneider
Lina Schneider

1 Best wishes
2 Yours faithfully
3 Dear Mrs Wilson
4 2nd May 2010
5 Dear Sir or Madam
6 I look forward to hearing from you.
7 I am writing to apply for the job of assistant receptionist as advertised on your website ...
8 Webergasse 8
81735 Munich
9 The Manager
Lancaster Hall Hotel
28 Lancaster Road
London W8 IJL

Tip 15

Note that in British addresses the house number comes **before** the name of the road or street, not after it.
Note also that in the UK the postcode comes **after** the town or city, not before it.

6621

c) *If **you** wanted this job, how would you write your letter of application? In your exercise book, write the main text of your letter. Include the following:*

- your personal details
- how long you have been learning English and how good your English is
- what kind of person you are, work experience, your hobbies and interests
- why you would like the job and why you think you could do it well.

[1] receptionist [rɪ'sepʃənɪst] *Empfangsmitarbeiter/in*

22 Writing a CV

► SF (p. 148)

Lina has to enclose her CV with the application. Here is the necessary information about her:

Her telephone number is 0049 89 612 37 97. Her mobile number is 0173 835 2380.
Her e-mail is: lschneider@afl.com
She was born in Munich on 23rd November 1995.

Lina is a friendly, hard-working student who likes speaking English and enjoys meeting people. She is good at organizing and likes working in a team. She is punctual and reliable.
She has already worked as a waitress[1] for six weeks in a hotel in Stockholm, Sweden, where she spoke English and German to hotel guests. Last year in the Easter holidays she also worked at the information desk in a shopping mall in Munich for two weeks.
In her free time she likes reading and writing to online friends in the UK and the USA. She enjoys cooking, swimming and playing tennis. She is a member of the school drama club.
Lina was at primary school in Augsburg from 2001 to 2005. She has been at secondary school in Munich since 2005. She is taking her school-leaving exams (similar to A-Levels) this year. She has a good level of everyday English (six years) and French (four years). She also has good computer skills and a moped licence.

a) *In what order should Lina present this information at the top of her CV? Write numbers 1–4 behind the headings.*

Postal address ..... E-mail address ..... Place of birth .....
Name ..... Mobile number ..... Date of birth .....

Tip 16

Date and place of birth are not always given in English CVs, but it is useful for employers to know your **age** and your **native language** if you are applying for a job abroad.
The **personal statement** should not be longer than three short sentences. Use only long verb forms.

b) *What could Lina write in her short personal statement?*

c) *In which order should she give details about the following? Write 1–6.*

Work experience ..... Hobbies and interests ..... Education .....
Qualifications ..... Reference(s) ..... Other skills .....

d) *Now use information in a) to write the CV sections in c), but leave out 'Reference(s)'. Remember to write notes, not full sentences.*

Education:

6722 **e)** *Write the CV on the computer using the correct format.*

[1] waitress ['weɪtrɪs] *Kellnerin*

SPEAKING

23 Asking for information (Question forms) ▸ WB (pp. 79–80) 29

When you ask for information, it is important to form questions correctly and quickly. How do the teenagers ask the questions below? Write in your exercise book. Then listen to your CD (29) to check your answers.

a) *Dana is at JFK airport in New York. She wants a bus to the town centre.*

She asks someone politely …
- *if they know where the buses leave from.*
- where the buses stop in the town centre.
- how long the bus ride takes.
- how much bus tickets cost.
- where you buy the bus tickets.

b) *Patrick is having an interview for a holiday job at a local IT company.*

He asks the interviewer …
- *what he would have to do exactly.*
- what time he would have to start.
- if he would have to work on Saturdays.
- how many hours he would have to work a week.
- when he could start.

6823

24 Describing a picture (Brainstorming vocabulary) ▸ WB (pp. 79–80) 30

When you describe a picture you usually have to …

- say generally where it is, e.g. *a scene in winter, a city street.*
- say where things/people are: *in the background/foreground/ middle, on the right/left, behind, in front of, between.*
- talk about the people (how many, what they are doing/wearing).
- say how the people are probably feeling or what they are thinking.
- use adjectives to talk about the atmosphere of the picture.

a) *Look at the picture below and in your exercise book, write down words to describe the scene. If you don't know the words you need, use your dictionary. Then describe the picture. You can record your speech.*

Tip 17

Useful phrases for talking about pictures:
- *The picture shows a scene in summer/at a beach/in a big city/in the mountains …*
- *It looks as if people are having fun …*
- *The girl/boy on the right is laughing/ chatting …*
- *Maybe she/he is thinking that …*
- *She might be …*
- *The people look/seem to be happy/ excited …*

Tip 18

Answering questions
Give your opinion and find reasons and arguments for it.
Here are some ideas:
- *I can't ski so I think summer holidays are better.*
- *In my opinion skiing holidays are too expensive …*
- *… I prefer holidays where I can …*
- *I like swimming and I'd like to learn to snowboard too because …*
- *Sport plays an important role in my free time. I … every week …*

b) *Be prepared to answer general questions that have to do with the picture indirectly. Listen to the questions on your CD (30). Answer each question with at least three complete sentences. You can make notes in your exercise book first. Then practise your answers, first from your notes, then without your notes. Concentrate on speaking clearly, not too quickly.*

25 Comparing pictures

▸ WB (pp. 79–80) 🎧 31

When you compare two pictures, talk about differences and compare advantages and disadvantages.

a) *Think of words and phrases to talk about the pictures below. Make lists:*

A

B

In a town	In the country
lots of people, cars, shops,	

Tip 19

General tips:
- Don't answer questions with just *Yes* or *No* only. Better: *Yes, I think so. No, I don't think so./ Yes, I do./Yes, it is. /No, it isn't, etc.*
- If you repeat an idea or opinion, say it differently.
- What you say should be good English without too many mistakes.

b) *Use your notes in a) to discuss the two pictures. You can record your speech.*

c) *You often have to discuss two pictures or a given topic with your exam partner. Your dialogue should be realistic, so ask relevant questions. Here are some questions that you could ask about the topic of this exercise. Ask these questions in English, then check them on your CD (🎧 31):*

1 Wohnst du in der Stadt oder auf dem Land?
2 Wie lange wohnst du schon dort?
3 Würdest du lieber irgendwo anders wohnen?
4 Wie kommst du in die Schule?
5 Wo wohnen deine Freunde?
6 Welche Vorteile hat man auf dem Land?
7 Welche Vorteile hat man in der Stadt?
8 Hast du irgendwelche Großstädte im Ausland besucht?
9 Welche Großstadt hat dir am besten gefallen?
10 Wenn du nicht in Deutschland wohntest, wo würdest du wohnen wollen?

d) **Extra** *Ask your partner the questions 3–10 in c).*

Tip 20

If you don't understand what the examiner/interviewer says, it's good to know some useful, polite **phrases** by heart.
- *Could you repeat that, please?*
- *Could you explain that again/once more, please?*
- *Sorry, I can't quite follow you.*
- *Do you mean that I have to ...?*
- *Sorry, what exactly do I have to do?*
- *Sorry, but I didn't quite understand/ catch what you said.*

Tip 21

Useful partner questions
When you have to talk to your exam partner, exchange information, give opinions, express feelings. You could start like this:
- *In my opinion, ...*
- *I have read that ...*
- *What do you think about ...?*
- *Don't you think that ...?*
- *Do you agree that ...?*
- *Isn't it better to ... than to ...?*
- *What's your opinion about ...?*

MEDIATION

26 London travel (Mediating a written text) ▸ WB (p. 79)

a) *You are going to visit London with your family and you want to tell them the best way to travel around the city. You find this information. Mark the main facts first. Then make notes below in German.*

Tip 22

Mark or underline the **main facts** and summarize them. Leave out details that are not important. Don't translate.

London Travelcards for international visitors

If you are planning to travel in and around London, it's best to buy a Travelcard. You will save money and you will have complete freedom[1] of travel on the Tube, buses, trams, Docklands Light Railway (DLR) and most local trains across the whole of London. You can even get riverboat tickets one third cheaper.

There are many different kinds of Travelcards. You have to choose whatever is best for you. You can buy a Travelcard for just one day, three days, seven days or even longer. London is divided into 6 travel zones and Travelcards cover different zones. Zones 1 and 2 cover Central London and most of the famous London sights. Zone 6 takes you to outer areas of the city. You must decide which zones you want to visit. Heathrow airport is in zone 6.

You must also know at what time you want to start your journey. If you plan to travel before 9.30 am (Mon–Fri), you will need a Peak Travelcard. If you travel after 9.30 am, you can buy an Off-Peak Travelcard, which is a little cheaper. For example, an Off-Peak One-day Travelcard for Zones 1 and 2 costs £5.60 for an adult (16 and over). By comparison, the Peak One-day Travelcard costs £7.20. Special reduced prices for children 5–15. Children under 5 go free. You can buy your Travelcard online, or all over the city at Tube stations, travel information centres and at some newsagents.

(Prices: 26.02.2010)

Tip 23

When you mediate written information, the order is not important. Before you start, find the main points. Sometimes it's easier to mark key words and note information under headings, here: **advantages, travel zones, journey times, prices.**

b) *You tell your parents what you have found out, but they still have a few questions. Give short answers in German.*

1 Wo kann man die *Travelcard* kaufen? ______

2 Kann man mit der *Travelcard* vom Flughafen in die Stadt fahren? ______

3 Du bist erst 16 und Schüler/in. Musst du schon den vollen Preis bezahlen? ______

4 Müssen wir für deinen Bruder zahlen? Er ist ja erst vier. ______

5 Wozu braucht man Zone 6? ______

[1] freedom ['fri:dəm] *Freiheit*

27 What did he say? (Mediating what you hear) ▸ WB (p. 79) 🎧 32

You are at home, listening to a music programme on the radio. Explain what you hear (🎧 32) to your American exchange student. Use your own words and tell your friend the main things in a few sentences. You can make notes while you are listening, especially dates, places, etc.

Tip 24

Listen for details: **dates, place names** (cities and countries). Don't mediate opinions of the presenter.
Make notes to help you remember.

Yes, he's talking about the 'Night Flyers'. They ______________________________

____

____

____

____

____

____

28 Explaining signs (Using modal auxiliaries) ▸ WB (p. 79)

You are in town with your dog, your bike and your British cousin. You want to explain these German signs to her. Complete with a modal (e. g. can, can't, must, mustn't, have to, etc.). More than one modal is sometimes possible.

Tip 25

Don't confuse ...!
you can't ...
du kannst/darfst nicht ...
you have to/you must ...
du musst ...
you don't have to .../you needn't ...
du musst/brauchst nicht ...
you mustn't ...
du darfst nicht ...

1  WIR MÜSSEN DRAUßEN BLEIBEN

We ______________________ take the dog in there.

2 PARKEN VERBOTEN Fahrräder bitte nicht abstellen!

You ______________________ park your bike here.

3 Ganztägig geöffnet Tischreservierung nicht erforderlich

You ______________________ book a table.

4 Konzertkarten Bitte anstellen[1]

You ______________ queue.

5 Betreten des Turms AUF EIGENE GEFAHR

You ______________________ go up the tower, but at your own risk.

6 RUHEZONE! MOBILTELEFONE BITTE AUSSCHALTEN!

You ______________ turn off your mobile.

7 STADTBIBLIOTHEK Haupteingang[2] wegen Renovierungsarbeiten geschlossen. Bitte Nebeneingang links um die Ecke benutzen.

We ______________________ use the main entrance.

We ______________ use the side entrance.

7128

[1] queue [kjuː] [2] main entrance ['meɪn entrəns]

LANGUAGE

29 A good story (Simple present or present progressive)

Trish is telling a friend about the film 'Australia'. Put the verbs in the simple present or present progressive.

'Well, the action takes place in northern Australia in 1939.

The war *is just starting* (just, start). Kidman ____________ (play) Lady Sarah Ashley, an English aristocrat whose husband ____________ (own) a huge farm and cattle station. Well, Sarah ____________ (fly) to Darwin to see what her husband ____________ (do) – she ____________ (believe) he ____________ (have) an affair.

When she ____________ (arrive), her husband's drover[1] ____________ (meet) her to take her to the farm – that's Jackman. On arrival they ____________ (find) her husband has been murdered, so now all the land ____________ (belong) to her. Someone ____________ (tell) her that the farm administrator[2] ____________ (steal) her cattle and ____________ (plan) to take over her land, so – oh, why ____________ (I, tell) you all this? You should see the film yourself.'

7229

Tip 26

Use the ***simple present*** (e. g. *he goes, I don't want*) for:
- summaries of stories, films and book reviews
- descriptions of characters in fictional texts
- comments on opinions/ideas
- your personal statement on your CV
- for talking about yourself and others; what you often do, what you like or don't like.

Use the ***present progressive*** (e. g. *he is going, I'm not going*) for actions and situations that are going on at the time. Remember, some verbs are not used in the progressive form: *believe, belong, know, like, need, own, seem.*

30 He didn't understand (Simple past or past progressive)

Complete with verbs in the simple past or past progressive.

Esra *wanted* (want) to improve her English, so she ____________ (apply) for a job as au pair in the USA.

She ____________ (not know) much about her American host family, but when she ____________ (arrive), all five members of her host family ____________ (wait) to meet her. While Esra ____________ (chat) to Mrs Jackson, Mr Jackson ____________ (pick) up her large bag, but Esra ____________ (say) loudly, 'Oh, no, Mr Jackson. You mustn't carry my bag.' So Mr Jackson suddenly ____________ (put) the bag down again. Why ____________ (Esra, want) to carry the heavy[3] bag herself? ____________ (she, have) something important in her bag, or something that might break? Mr Jackson ____________ (not say) anything. When they ____________ (walk) out of the airport, Esra ____________ (think), 'Why ____________ (he, put) my bag down? Was it too heavy for him? What was the problem?' Do you know?

7230

Tip 27

Use the ***simple past*** (e. g. *went, didn't go*) for completed actions in the past, often with signal words - *yesterday, last year*, etc. Use it in stories or reports, or to talk about *when* something happened in the past.
Make questions and negatives with ***did***.
Use the ***past progressive*** (e. g. *was dancing, weren't eating*) for actions that were going on and not completed at a time in the past, for example, to describe a scene.

[1] drover [drəʊvə] *Viehhirte* [2] administrator [əd'mɪnɪstreɪtə] *Verwalter/in* [3] heavy ['hevɪ] *schwer*

31 Using different words (Synonyms)

a) Find and write pairs of words with similar meaning.

afraid • allow • almost • awful • brilliant • close to • connect • dependable • discover • fantastic • find • impolite • latest • let • link • most modern • near • nearly • reliable • rescue • rude • sad • save • scared • strange • terrible • unhappy • unusual

afraid – scared, __________

____

____

b) Where can you use a synonym? Mark the word that you can replace. Then rewrite it.

1 Sylvie is training to be a bank clerk[1] in a bank near the town centre. ➜ close to

2 Her boss is very strict. He doesn't let his workers leave work early. ➜ __________

3 Today Sylvie has almost finished her work. ➜ __________

4 She is a good worker and very dependable. ➜ __________

5 She would like to leave early, but she is afraid the boss will be angry. ➜ __________

6 The last time that someone wanted to leave early the boss was very impolite. ➜ __________

7 One day Sylvie found some documents – in the bin in her boss's office. ➜ __________

7331 8 The next day, the boss asked Sylvie if she would like to leave early – how strange! ➜ __________

32 Saying it differently (Changing sentence structure)

Tip 28

It is important to use your own words when you:
- write a summary.
- mediate what someone says.
- answer questions about a text.
- take notes from a written text.

Use the word in brackets to express the meaning in a different way.

1 The phone rang while Mel was watching her favourite soap. (during)

The phone rang during Mel's favourite soap.

2 It was her boyfriend. The last time she had seen him was three days ago. (for)

She hadn't __________

3 'Come to see the new film at the Majestic with me,' he said. (wanted)

He __________

4 The cinema was full, but they were able to find some seats. (although)

____

5 The film wasn't as bad as the last one they had seen. (better)

____

[1] bank clerk [klɑːk] *Bankangestellte/r*

33 The flying doctors of Australia (RFDS) (Using linking words)

▸ WB (p. 82)

Join two sentences with the linking word in brackets. Change the order of the sentences only where necessary.

Tip 29

Linking words are important in written English. They improve the style of your texts – and get you better marks in exams! Make sure that you use them whenever possible.

1 About 10% of Australians live far away from towns and cities. They can't get medical help easily. (so)

About 10% of Australians live… cities, so they can't get medical help easily.

2 Before the RFDS started, many people died. Doctors could not reach them. (because)

3 The Service is very well organized. It can reach people in over 80% of the country. (so)

4 The RFDS has set up more than 20 bases[1] all over the country. Doctors can reach people quickly. (so that)

5 It is not easy to pass the tests and interviews. Lots of young people apply to the RFDS. (although)

6 The RFDS was started in about 1930. The RFDS is a 24-hour service. (which)

7433

34 Explaining words (Paraphrasing)

▸ WB (p. 79)

If you don't know the English word for what you want to say, you can paraphrase it. Paraphrasing is useful in mediation. You are talking to your English cousin about jobs and workplaces. Explain the following words in English. You can use these phrases:

- *It's someone/a person who … It's something that …*
- *It's something you use to … It's a place where …*
- *It's a (general word) that …*

I'd like to be a – erm, in German it's 'Regisseur'. *It's someone who knows a lot about film-making and directs films.*

1 Arbeitgeber/in:

2 Bewerbungsschreiben:

3 Lebenslauf:

4 Führerschein:

7434

[1] base [beɪs] *Stützpunkt*

35 Making texts more interesting (Using adjectives)

a) *Choose three adjectives from the box that you could use in 1–4 below. Some adjectives fit into more than one list. Then add at least two more suitable adjectives to each list.*

boring • busy • clean • dangerous • exciting • healthy • interesting • noisy • polite • serious • quiet • reliable

1 a job: __________

2 a town/city: __________

3 the countryside[1]: __________

4 a job candidate: __________

b) *Write one or two sentences each about 1–4 in a). Use as many adjectives as you can from the lists.*

1 *I would like to have a job that's interesting and* __________

2 __________

3 __________

4 __________

36 She wanted to know ... (Indirect questions)

Jenny had an interview for a job as flight attendant[2]. She had some questions about the training course. What did she want to know? Report her questions.

Jenny asked/wanted to know ...

Tip 30

It is polite to use indirect questions in formal letters:
Could you please let me know whether/ when/where/who ...
Remember the backshift of tenses.

1 *how long the course was.*

2 __________

3 __________

4 __________

5 __________

6 __________

7 __________

7536 8 __________

1 *How long is the course?*
2 Where do the courses take place?
3 What are the course hours?
4 What will I learn on the course?
5 Will the instruction be in English?
6 Will I have to take any tests?
7 How many others will be on the course?
8 Will I get any money during training?

[1] countryside *(auf dem) Land* [2] flight attendant ['flaɪt əˌtendənt] *Flugbegleiter/in*

37 About Simon (Word order in subordinate clauses)

> **Tip 31**
> Word order in English is different from German. It is always **Subject-Verb-Object**.
> Compare:
> Since S. **left** *school* he has ...
> *Seitdem S. die Schule* **verließ**, *hat er ...*

Write down the words of the subordinate clauses in the right order.

1 [Since] [school] [Simon] [left], he has been working as a trainee[1] in a local bank.

Since Simon left school, he has been working ...

2 Simon plays football for the local team, so [has to] [he] [regularly] [twice a week] [train].

... ______

3 If [well] [he] [works], the manager lets him go home earlier.

______, ...

4 That's usually on the days when [has to] [he] [to] [football training] [go].

... ______

5 Sometimes the manager lets him leave early, [he] [his work] [hasn't finished] [although].

... ______

6 The manager lets him go early because [of the local team] [he] [too] [is] [a big supporter].

... ______

38 A trip to New York (Correcting your text) ▸ WB (p. 82)

> **Tip 32**
> **Last but not least:**
> Always remember to read your texts carefully as soon as you finish them. Checking for mistakes is a very important part of any written task. Good luck!

Correct Lina's e-mail to her online friend in Washington. Look for wrong words, wrong spelling (e.g. ~~planing~~) and grammar mistakes.

Hi Kelly!
Here we are in New York! It's so cool here. I really enjoyed ~~planing~~ our sightseeing tour befor we came and we've done the most of the things on my list. We've been in New York since two days. The whether was great yesterday, so we have gone up the Empire State Building. I made some pretty cool photos and I heared many informations over the details of the building. We all have thought that it was really intresting. The american peoples are very friendly and helpfull. They always say me what I want to know. New York isn't so far from Washington. Maybe I could travell down to Washington with the train to see you for a day or two. Would that be OK? I'm calling you this evening. Than you can tell me what you mean. If I would come to visit you, I'm sure we had lots of fun! Lina

Correct

planning,

______

______

______

______

7638

[1] trainee [treɪˈniː] *Auszubildende/r*

LISTENING SKILLS

SF REVISION Listening ▶ *p. 134*

Vor dem Hören

- Frag dich, was du schon über das Thema weißt.
- Nutze Überschriften oder Bilder, um zu erahnen, was dich z. B. bei einer Geschichte erwarten könnte.
- Lies dir die Aufgaben auf deinem Aufgabenblatt genau durch und überlege, auf welche Informationen du dich konzentrieren musst.
- Bereite dich darauf vor, Notizen zu machen. Leg z. B. eine Tabelle oder Liste an.

Während des Hörens

Listening for gist:
Konzentriere dich beim ersten Hören auf allgemeine Informationen, z. B. die Personen (unterschiedliche Stimmen), das Thema, die Umgebung (Geräusche), die Atmosphäre (die Sprechweise der Leute).

Listening for detail:

- Mach dir noch einmal bewusst, worauf du genau achten willst (Hörauftrag), besonders bei Durchsagen (*announcements*), die du vielleicht nur einmal hören kannst.
- Gerate nicht in Panik, wenn du meinst, du hättest gerade etwas Wichtiges verpasst. Konzentriere dich auf die nächste wichtige Information.
- Lass dich nicht von anderen Einzelheiten oder Geräuschen ablenken.
- Mach nur kurze Notizen, z. B. Anfangsbuchstaben, Symbole oder Stichworte.
- Manche Signalwörter machen es dir leichter, den Hörtext zu verstehen.
  Aufzählung: **and**, **another**, **too**
  Gegensatz: **although**, **but**
  Grund, Folge: **because**, **so**, **so that**
  Vergleich: **larger/older/... than**, **as ... as**, **more**, **most**
  Reihenfolge: **before**, **after**, **then**, **next**, **later**, **when**, **at last**, **at the same time**
- Auch andere Details wie z.B. die Stimme, der Akzent oder der Tonfall des Sprechers oder der Sprecherin können dir helfen, Informationen über seine oder ihre Gefühle, Herkunft usw. zu bekommen.
- Unterteile Telefonnummern beim Aufschreiben: 0171 572 42 589.

Nach dem Hören

- Vervollständige deine Notizen sofort.
- Wenn du den Text ein zweites Mal hören kannst, konzentriere dich auf das, was du beim ersten Mal nicht genau verstanden hast.
- Schau dir noch einmal die Aufgabenstellung an. Sollst du die gehörten Informationen nutzen, um einen neuen Text zu schreiben? Dann achte auf die richtige Textform: Bericht, Beschreibung, ...

REVISION Reading course – Zusammenfassung

Working out the meaning of words ▶ *p. 136*

Das Nachschlagen unbekannter Wörter im Wörterbuch kostet Zeit und nimmt auf Dauer den Spaß am Lesen. Oft geht es auch ohne Wörterbuch:

1. Bilder und Zeichen erklären und ergänzen oft Dinge aus dem Text. Schau sie dir deshalb vor und nach dem Lesen genau an.
2. Manche Wörter erklären sich aus dem Textzusammenhang, z.B. *When we **reached** the station, Judy bought our tickets.*
3. Zu manchen englischen Wörtern fallen dir vielleicht deutsche, französische oder lateinische Wörter ein, die ähnlich geschrieben oder ausgesprochen werden, z. B. **excellent**, **millionaire**, **nation**, **reality**.
4. Es gibt neue Wörter, in denen du bekannte Teile entdeckst, z. B. **friendliness**, **helpless**, **understandable**, **gardener**, **tea bag**, **waiting room**.

Skimming and scanning ► *p. 136*

Beim **Skimming** überfliegst du einen Text schnell, um dir einen **Überblick** zu verschaffen. Du willst dabei herausfinden, worum es in dem Text geht. Achte dabei auf

- die **Überschrift**,
- die **Zwischenüberschriften** und hervorgehobene Wörter oder Sätze,
- die **Bilder** und **Bildunterschriften**,
- den **ersten Satz** und den **letzten Satz** jedes Absatzes,
- **Grafiken**, **Statistiken** und die **Quelle** des Textes.

Beim **Scanning** suchst du nach **bestimmten Informationen**. Dazu suchst du den Text nach Schlüsselwörtern (*key words*) ab und liest nur dort genauer, wo du sie findest. Geh dabei so vor:

Schritt 1: Denk an die Schlüsselwörter und geh mit deinen Augen oder dem Finger schnell durch den Text, in breiten Schlingen wie bei einem „S" oder „Z" oder von oben nach unten wie bei einem „U". Die gesuchten Wörter werden dir sofort „ins Auge springen".

Schritt 2: Wenn das gesuchte Wort nicht im Text vorkommt, überlege dir andere, themenverwandte Wörter (z. B. **lesson** → **school**, **subject**) und suche nach diesen.

Finding the main ideas of a text ► *p. 136*

Zeitungsartikel, Berichte oder Kommentare verstehst du besser, wenn du ihre wesentlichen Aussagen erkennst und dir klar machst, wie sie zusammenhängen. Die wichtigsten Aussagen findest du so:

1. Jeder Text hat ein Thema mit mindestens einer Hauptaussage, z. B.:
   Drinking soda is one of the worst things you can do to your health.
   Diese Hauptaussage findest du oft im **ersten Absatz**.
2. Die Hauptaussage wird in der Regel durch weitere Aussagen bzw. Gedanken unterstützt, z. B.:
   Experts agree that sugary soft drinks and fast food are the main reasons why so many American teenagers are fat.
3. Diese weiteren Aussagen bzw. Gedanken werden oft durch Beispiele und Begründungen ergänzt, z. B.:
   About 7% of the calories that they take in come from soft drinks alone.

Careful reading ► *p. 137*

Schwierige Texte musst du besonders sorgfältig und konzentriert lesen, damit du alle darin enthaltenen Informationen und Gedanken verstehst.

1. Lies den Text genau. Welches sind seine wesentlichen Aussagen? (► *Finding the main ideas of a text, s. oben*)
2. Manchmal musst du dir die Antwort auf eine Frage aus einzelnen Informationen erschließen, die du an verschiedenen Stellen im Text findest. Nimm zum Beispiel den Text auf S. 17 in deinem SB: Warum ist in der Überschrift von einem „racist ideal" die Rede?
   Für die Antwort musst du mehrere Aussagen aus dem Text zusammentragen:

FACTS: • *Zita Wallace and thousands of other mixed-race children with fair skin were taken from their Aboriginal families.* • *The government wanted them to forget their Aboriginal traditions and grow up like white children.* • *The children were hit if they spoke their own language.* • *They had to work all the time and didn't get any real education.*

CONCLUSION: The government thought that Aboriginal culture had no value. The mixed-race children were forced to grow up among white people, but at the same time they were discriminated against.

Text types: fiction and non-fiction ► *p. 137*

Wenn du einen Text liest, ist es sinnvoll sich klar zu machen, ob er von einer vom Autor erdachten Welt handelt (*fictional text*, deutsch: Dichtung) oder sich mit der Wirklichkeit auseinandersetzt (*non-fictional text*, deutsch: Sachtext).

Fiktionale Texte sind z. B. Kurzgeschichten und Romane. Der Autor wählt Figuren (*characters*) aus und erzählt von ihren Gefühlen und Handlungen, von deren Motiven und Hintergründen. Die Handlungen finden in einem oder mehreren Handlungsrahmen statt, z. B. an einem Ort, zu einer bestimmten Zeit und unter bestimmten Umständen (*setting*). Die Ereignisse können aus verschiedenen Perspektiven erzählt werden (*point of view*). Oft verwendet der Autor für seine Geschichte eine anschauliche Sprache, z. B. ausschmückende Adjektive, Metaphern, Vergleiche, direkte Rede oder er lässt den Leser an den Gedanken seiner Figuren oder des Erzählers teilhaben.

Nicht-fiktionale Texte sind z. B. Berichte in Zeitungen, wissenschaftliche Artikel, Aufsätze oder Kommentare. Hier informiert der Autor über ein Thema der realen Welt oder nimmt Stellung dazu.

Es gibt auch Texte, die eine **Mischform** aus beiden Textarten sind.

MEDIATION SKILLS

SF REVISION Mediation ▸ p. 140

REVISION Wann muss ich zwischen zwei Sprachen vermitteln?

Manchmal musst du zwischen zwei Sprachen vermitteln. Das nennt man **mediation**.

1. Du gibst englische Informationen auf Deutsch weiter: Du fährst z.B. mit deiner Familie in die USA und deine Eltern oder Geschwister wollen wissen, was jemand in einem Café gesagt hat oder was an einer Informationstafel steht.
2. Du gibst deutsche Informationen auf Englisch weiter: Vielleicht ist bei dir zu Hause eine Austauschschülerin aus den USA oder Dänemark zu Gast, die kein Deutsch spricht und Hilfe braucht.
3. In schriftlichen Prüfungen musst du manchmal in einem englischen Text gezielt nach Informationen suchen und diese auf Deutsch wiedergeben. Oder du sollst Informationen aus einem deutschen Text auf Englisch wiedergeben.

Worauf muss ich bei *mediation* achten?

- Übersetze nicht alles wörtlich, sondern gib den Sinn wieder.
- Gib nur das Wesentliche weiter, lass Unwichtiges weg.
- Verwende kurze und einfache Sätze.
- Wenn du ein Wort nicht kennst, umschreibe es oder ersetze es durch ein anderes Wort.

Was kann ich tun, wenn ich ein wichtiges Wort nicht kenne?

Vielleicht findest du es manchmal schwer, mündliche Aussagen oder schriftliche Textvorlagen in die andere Sprache zu übertragen, z.B. weil

- dein Wortschatz nicht ausreicht,
- dir bekannte Wörter „im Stress" nicht einfallen,
- spezielle Fachbegriffe auftauchen.

Manche Wörter kannst du umschreiben, z.B. mithilfe von Relativsätzen wie:
It's somebody/a person who ...
It's something that you use to ...
It's an animal that ...
It's a place that/where ...
Schau dir auch unten auf dieser Seite den Abschnitt zu Paraphrasing an.

SPEAKING AND WRITING SKILLS

SF REVISION Paraphrasing ▸ p. 141

Worum geht es beim Paraphrasing?

„Paraphrasing" bedeutet, etwas mit anderen Worten zu erklären. Das ist hilfreich, wenn dir ein bestimmtes Wort nicht einfällt oder wenn dein Gegenüber dich nicht verstanden hat. Paraphrasing ist auch besonders nützlich für **mediation** (▸ *Mediation, s. oben*).

Wie gehe ich beim Paraphrasing vor?

- Man kann mit einem Ausdruck umschreiben, der dieselbe Bedeutung hat: **'To wonder' is the same as 'to ask yourself'.** Oder man sagt das Gegenteil: **'Alive' is the opposite of 'dead'.**
- Manchmal braucht man mehrere Wörter, z.B. wenn man etwas beschreibt oder erklären will, wie man etwas verwendet. Dabei verwendet man ein allgemeines Wort (**general word**) und nennt weitere Eigenschaften: **A skyscraper is a very tall building.**
- Oder du umschreibst das Wort mit **... is/are like ...** **A lodge is like a small house or cabin. You find it in the country.**
- Du kannst auch einen Relativsatz (**relative clause**) verwenden: **A ticket office is a shop where you can buy tickets for shows and concerts.**

SF REVISION Brainstorming ▸ p. 141

Was ist Brainstorming und wofür ist es gut?

Bei vielen Aufgaben ist es nützlich, wenn du im ersten Schritt möglichst viele Ideen zum Thema sammelst. Beim Sammeln und beim Auswerten der Ideen helfen dir die folgenden Techniken.

Drei verschiedene Brainstorming-Techniken

Technik 1: Making a list

Schreib die Ideen so auf, wie sie dir einfallen, und zwar für jede Idee eine neue Zeile. Lies im zweiten Schritt alle deine Ideen durch. Überlege, welche Ideen davon für dein Thema sinnvoll sind und nummeriere sie nach Nützlichkeit.

Technik 2: Making a mind map

Leg eine Mindmap an. Überlege dafür, welche Oberbegriffe zu deinem Thema passen. Verwende unterschiedliche Farben für jeden Oberbegriff. Ergänze jede Idee, die zu einem Oberbegriff passt, auf einem Nebenast. Nimm dafür nur wichtige Schlüsselwörter. Du kannst statt Wörtern auch Symbole verwenden und Bilder ergänzen.

Technik 3: The 5 Ws

Schreib die Fragewörter Who? What? When? Where? Why? in eine Tabelle. Die Ideen, die dir zu der jeweiligen Frage kommen, werden darunter geschrieben.

SPEAKING COURSE – Zusammenfassung

Having a conversation ▸ p. 142

Ein Gespräch beginnen

Ein Gespräch auf Englisch zu beginnen ist einfacher, als du vielleicht denkst. Es gibt immer mehrere Möglichkeiten:

- **Wenn du etwas erfragen willst** (z.B. den Weg oder die Uhrzeit) **oder um Hilfe bitten möchtest:** Excuse me, do you know ... • Excuse me, can you tell me ... • Excuse me, do you know where... • Could you help me, please?
- **Wenn du jemanden begrüßen möchtest oder kennen lernst:** Hi! • Hello! • Good morning. • (bei Erwachsenen) Good afternoon. Oft kann man das Gespräch dann mit einer allgemeinen Bemerkung weiterführen: Great day today! • Nice concert, isn't it? • ... Oft hört man zur Begrüßung auch: How are you? oder How do you do? Das sind einfache Begrüßungsformeln, auf die keine Antwort erwartet wird. Am besten sagst du einfach: Fine, thanks. How about you?
- **Wenn du jemanden wiedertriffst:** Hi, ..., how are things? • Hi, how is it going? • How are you? • Hi, good to see/meet you.

Ein Gespräch führen

Für den weiteren Verlauf des Gesprächs sind diese Wendungen nützlich:

- **Sich vorstellen:** By the way, my name's ... • I'm ...
- **Sich kennen lernen:** Have you ... before? • Have you ever ...? • What about you?
- **Sich bedanken/auf einen Dank reagieren:** Thanks! • Thanks for your help. • You're welcome.
- **Sich verabschieden:** See you tomorrow/next week. • Bye!

Und wenn du einmal etwas nicht verstanden hast, kannst du nachfragen:
Sorry, I didn't get that. • Sorry, can you say that again, please?

Asking for, confirming, giving information ▸ p. 142

Ein Gespräch ist mehr als nur der Austausch von Informationen; es kommt auch auf einen höflichen und angenehmen Ton an. Das gilt natürlich auch für Gespräche auf Englisch. Diese Wendungen können hilfreich sein:

- **Asking for information:** Oft beginnt man eine Anfrage oder Auskunft mit: Excuse me... • Excuse me, could you tell me, ... • Would you mind telling me ... • Sorry, I'd just like to know... • I'm not quite sure about ... • Is it/Are they ...? • Is it right that ...? • Can I just ask ... • Excuse me, I've just got a question ... • Excuse me, do you think you could ...?
- **Confirming information:** Wenn du nachfragen oder sichergehen möchtest, dass du etwas richtig verstanden hast, kannst du das z.B. so tun: Can I just confirm ...? • Is it right that ...? • Have I got that right ...? • ..., (is that) right? • Could you just say that again, please? Auch *question tags* drücken den Wunsch nach Bestätigung aus: This is the library, isn't it?

Denke auch daran, dich für die erhaltenen Informationen freundlich zu bedanken.

- **Giving information:** Auch wenn du selbst eine Auskunft erteilst, versuche freundlich und höflich zu sein, z.B. mit einer kurzen Einleitung: **Sure.** • **Of course, no problem.** • **Well, just a second.** • **Give me a minute to think about it.** Wenn du nicht weiter helfen kannst, drückst du dein Bedauern aus: **Oh, I'm sorry, I don't know.** • **Sorry, I'm afraid I can't help you.**

Giving an oral summary ▸ *p. 143*

Wenn du etwas, was du gehört, gesehen oder gelesen hast, für jemanden anderen zusammenfassen willst, tust du dies oft spontan. Du hast also nicht lange Zeit zum Überlegen und solltest auch nicht zu lange reden.

- Gib **nur das Wesentliche** des Inhalts wieder. Du brauchst dich nicht unbedingt an die chronologische Reihenfolge der Handlung zu halten: **I watched that film ... last night.** • **Yesterday I read that web article about ...** • **I've recently come across that ad/article about ...** • **I've just read that story about ...**
- Verwende das **Präsens** zum Nacherzählen: **There's this kid ... In this one scene he's running away from ... then it starts raining ... and he's trying ... so she has to get out of the car ...**
- **Halte deine Meinung** zu dem betreffenden Film, Buch usw. **zurück**. Natürlich kannst du durch die Art und Weise, wie du erzählst, indirekt deinen Eindruck wiedergeben, z.B. durch den Ton deiner Stimme, deine Körpersprache und deine Wortwahl.

Having a discussion ▸ *p. 143*

Seine Meinung sagen und erklären

- **Expressing an opinion:** In einer Diskussion ist es gut, wenn du möglichst klar und deutlich sagst, was du zu einer bestimmten Frage denkst: **I think ...** • **I feel ...** • **In my opinion ...**
- **Giving reasons and examples**: Es ist aber noch wichtiger, dass du Beispiele und Argumente nennst, die deine Meinung unterstützen – schließlich willst du deine Gesprächspartner ja überzeugen: **because ...** • **First ... / Second ...** • **For example ...** • **Let me explain ...** • **That's why ...**

Auf andere reagieren

- **Asking for clarification:** Manchmal ist es notwendig nachzuhaken: **Could you say that again?** • **Sorry, but I don't understand what you mean.**
- **Agreeing with someone:** Die Meinung eines anderen unterstützt du mit: **I agree (with you/...).** • **That's a good point.** • **You're right.**
- **Disagreeing with someone:** Oft widerspricht man nicht direkt, sondern leitet seine Reaktion z.B. mit **Sorry, ...** ein. Zeig immer Respekt für die Meinung anderer: **I don't think you can say ...** • **I see what you mean but ...** • **No, that's not right.** • **Sorry, I don't agree with you.** • **Yes, but ...,** • **Well, I don't think you can say that ...** • **Ah, come on, ...**

REVISION Writing course – Zusammenfassung

The steps of writing

1. Brainstorming – Ideen sammeln und ordnen (▸ *Brainstorming, p. 80*)

2. Schreiben. Dabei achte darauf,
- deine Sätze zu verbinden und auszubauen (*Writing better sentences*),
- deinen Text gut zu strukturieren (*Using paragraphs*),
- bei einem Bericht die 5 Ws abzudecken (*Writing a report*),
- bei einem Leserbrief an eine Zeitschrift eine höfliche Anrede und Schlussformel zu verwenden (*Writing a letter to a magazine*).

3. Deinen Text inhaltlich und sprachlich überprüfen (*Correcting your text*)

Writing better sentences ▸ *p. 144*

Linking words verbinden Sätze und machen sie interessanter. Verwende z. B.
- **Time phrases** wie **at 7 o'clock**, **every morning**, **in the afternoon**, **a few minutes later**, **suddenly**, **then**, **next ...**,
- **Konjunktionen** wie **although**, **and**, **because**, **but**, **so ... that**, **that**, **when**, **while**,
- **Relativpronomen** wie **who**, **which** und **that**.

Auch mit **Adjektiven** und **Adverbien** kannst du deine Sätze verbessern.

- **Adjektive** bestimmen Personen, Orte, Gegenstände oder Erlebnisse genauer und machen sie ebenfalls interessanter: **The man looked into the room.** → **The young man looked into the empty room.**
- Mit **Adverbien** kannst du beschreiben, wie jemand etwas macht: **The young man looked nervously into the empty room.**

Using paragraphs ▸ *p. 144*

Structuring a text

Einen Text versteht man viel besser, wenn er in Absätze gegliedert ist:

- eine Einleitung (**beginning**) – hier schreibst du, worum es geht,
- einen Hauptteil (**middle**) – hier schreibst du mehr über dein Thema,
- einen Schluss (**end**) – hier bringst du den Text zu einem interessanten Ende.

Am Anfang eines Absatzes sind kurze, einleitende Sätze (**topic sentences**) gut, die den Lesern sofort sagen, worum es geht, z. B.

- Orte: **My trip to ... was fantastic. / ... is famous for ... / ... is a great place.**
- Personen: **... is great/funny/interesting/clever/...**
- Aktivitäten: **... is great fun. / Lots of people ... every day.**

Wie kann ich meine Absätze interessant gestalten?

- Beginne mit einem interessanten Einstiegssatz: **Guess what happened to me today! / Did I tell you that ...?**
- Fang für jeden neuen Aspekt einen neuen Absatz an.
- Beende deinen Text mit einer Zusammenfassung oder etwas Persönlichem.

Linking ideas

Damit sich dein Text flüssig liest und beim Leser Interesse weckt, solltest du auf gute Übergange von einem Absatz zum nächsten achten. Die folgenden Formulierungen kannst du verwenden,

- um zu zeigen, wie dein Text aufgebaut ist: **In the article, the writer describes how ... Firstly, he states that ... Secondly, ... Then he goes on to say that ... Another point he makes is that ... Finally, ...**
- um etwas zu begründen: **Because of / As a result of the growing population, ... had been in trouble with the police, so ...**
- um zwei oder mehr Gedanken einander gegenüberzustellen: **Although one could say that ..., I believe ... While most people would ..., the Prime Minister has said ... Serious scientists all say that ... However/But some politicians ...**
- um Beispiele zu geben: **This is true in a number of cases, for example / for instance / e.g. ...**
- um Ergebnisse und Folgen zu erklären: **As a consequence, / All in all, one can say that ... To sum up, I would like to say ...**

Correcting your text ▸ *p. 145*

Lies jeden Text, den du geschrieben hast, mehrmals durch,

- um zu sehen, ob er vollständig und gut verständlich ist,
- um ihn auf Fehler zu überprüfen, z. B. **Rechtschreibfehler *(spelling mistakes)*** und **Grammatikfehler *(grammar mistakes)***.

Spelling mistakes

Beachte folgende Regeln:

- Manche Wörter haben Buchstaben, die man nicht spricht, aber schreibt, z. B. **talk**, **climb**.
- Manchmal ändert sich die Schreibweise, wenn ein Wort eine Endung erhält, z. B. **take** → **taking**, **terrible** → **terribly**, **lucky** → **luckily**, **try** → **tries** (aber **stay** → **stays**), **run** → **running**, **drop** → **dropped**.
- Beim Plural tritt manchmal noch ein *-e* zum *-s*, z. B. **church** → **churches**.

Grammar mistakes

Diese Tipps helfen dir, typische Fehler zu vermeiden:

- Im **simple present** wird in der 3. Person Singular **-s** angehängt: **she knows**.
- **Unregelmäßige Verben**: Manche Verben bilden die Formen des *simple past* und des Partizip Perfekt *(past participle)* unregelmäßig. Die unregelmäßigen Formen musst du lernen, z. B. **go – went – gone**; **buy – bought – bought**. Die Liste steht im SB auf S. 240–241.
- **Verneinung**: Im *simple present* werden Vollverben mit **don't/doesn't** verneint, im *simple past* mit **didn't**.
- **Satzstellung**: Im Englischen gilt immer (auch im Nebensatz):

a) subject – verb – object (SVO): **... when I saw my brother.**
... als ich meinen Bruder sah.

b) Orts- vor Zeitangabe: **I bought a nice book in the city yesterday.**

GF 1 The *to*-infinitive

► *pp. 154–155*

1.1 REVISION Verb + object + *to*-infinitive

Kim **helped** me to write my French essay.
Kim half mir, meinen französischen Aufsatz zu schreiben.
Sharon **asked** me not to use her photo.
Sharon bat mich, ihr Foto nicht zu verwenden.

◄ Nach bestimmten Verben kann ein **Objekt + *to*-Infinitiv** stehen, z. B. ***ask/help/force/teach sb. (not) to do sth***.
Nach den entsprechenden deutschen Verben steht meist ein Infinitiv mit „zu“:
jn. bitten/jm. helfen/..., etwas (nicht) zu tun.

They **told** us to get into the truck.
Sie sagten, dass wir in den LKW einsteigen sollten.
The government **wanted** them to forget their traditions.
... wollte, dass sie ihre Traditionen vergessen.
Wallace **would like** the government to apologize.
... möchte, dass sich die Regierung entschuldigt.

◄ Auch nach den Verben ***cause, expect, tell, want, would like, would love*** kann ein **Objekt + *to*-Infinitiv** stehen.

! Nach den entsprechenden deutschen Verben steht ein Nebensatz mit „dass“. Auf die englischen Verben darf jedoch kein *that*-Satz folgen:
*Wir **wollen**, dass du uns hilfst.* *We **want** you to help us.*
Nicht: *We want ~~that you help~~ us.*

1.2 REVISION Question word + *to*-infinitive

We **don't know** what to do.
(... what we should/could do)
Wir wissen nicht, was wir tun sollen/könnten.
Let's **ask** someone how to get to the bus station.
..., wie wir zum Busbahnhof kommen (können).
They **wondered** whether to go or to stay.
..., ob sie gehen oder bleiben sollten.
I'm not sure which direction to take.
..., welche Richtung ich nehmen soll/muss.

Der *to*-Infinitiv steht oft nach einem **Fragewort** (*what, who, when, where, how* usw.) sowie nach *whether* („ob“). Er entspricht meist einem Nebensatz mit modalem Hilfsverb *(can, could, might, must, should)*.

Die Kombination aus Fragewort und *to*-Infinitiv steht oft nach den Verben *ask, explain, find out, know, show, tell, wonder* und nach *I'm not sure*.

1.3 The *to*-infinitive instead of a relative clause

1 Zita wasn't **the first (girl)** to cry.
(... the first girl who cried)
We're **the only shop** to offer this service.
(... the only shop that offers this service)
Sophie was **the only person/the only one** to say what she thought.
(... the only person/one who said ...)

2 Who was **the youngest (girl or boy)** to take part in the competition?
(... the youngest girl or boy who took ...)

Der *to*-Infinitiv kann **anstelle eines Relativsatzes** stehen

1 nach *the first, the last, the next, the only*.

! Nach *the only* muss ein Nomen oder *one/ones* stehen.

2 nach einem Superlativ.

1 There were hard **mattresses** to sleep on.
(... mattresses that we/they could sleep on)
Philip is **the person** to ask about grammar.
(... the person who you should ask)
2 There was **no one** to help us.
(... no one who could help us)
I'm looking for **someone** to share a flat with.
(... someone who I can share a flat with)

Der *to*-Infinitiv kann **anstelle eines Relativsatzes <u>mit modalem Hilfsverb</u>** stehen
1 nach einem **Nomen** (häufig nach *person, place, way*).
2 nach den Zusammensetzungen mit ***some-, any-*** und ***no-*** (*someone, something, somewhere, anybody, no one, nowhere* usw.).

GF 2 The gerund

► *pp. 156–157*

2.1 REVISION The gerund as subject and object

Subject	**Object**
Riding is fun.	I love riding.
Reiten macht Spaß.	Ich liebe das Reiten. / Ich reite sehr gern.

Wenn die *-ing*-Form eines Verbs die Funktion eines **Nomens** hat, wird sie **Gerundium** *(gerund)* genannt.
Das Gerundium kann **Subjekt** oder **Objekt** eines Satzes sein.

I like **riding my bike.** Ich fahre gern Rad.
Cycling in the rain can be fun too.
Radfahren im Regen kann auch Spaß machen. /
Im Regen Rad zu fahren kann auch Spaß machen.

Wie ein Verb kann das Gerundium erweitert werden, z.B. durch ein Objekt (hier: *my bike*) oder eine Orts- oder Zeitangabe (hier: *in the rain*).

1 Nobody **enjoys** going to the dentist's.
Niemand geht gern zum Zahnarzt.
Imagine living in California!
Stell dir vor, in Kalifornien zu leben!
Tom **suggested** going for an ice cream.
Tom schlug vor, ein Eis essen zu gehen.

! Beachte:

◂ **1** Nach einigen Verben – z.B. ***avoid, dislike, enjoy, fancy, finish, imagine, miss, practise, suggest*** – muss ein weiteres Verb als Gerundium stehen: *I* ***enjoy*** *going ...; He* ***suggested*** *going ...*
Anders als im Deutschen darf nach diesen Verben **kein Infinitiv** stehen!
Also nicht: *I ~~enjoy to go~~ ...; He ~~suggested to go~~ ...*

2 When it **started** raining / to rain we all went home.
Als es anfing zu regnen, gingen wir alle nach Haus.

◂ **2** Nach ***begin/start, continue, hate, like, love, prefer*** kann jedoch – bei gleicher Bedeutung – entweder ein Gerundium oder ein *to*-Infinitiv stehen.

3 I'll never **forget** talking to Robbie Williams.
Ich werde nie vergessen, wie ich mit Robbie Williams gesprochen habe.
I **forgot** to phone Grandpa. I'm sorry.
Ich habe vergessen, Opa anzurufen. Es tut mir leid.

I **remember** posting the letter last Friday.
Ich erinnere mich daran, letzten Freitag den Brief eingeworfen zu haben.
I must **remember** to post this card tomorrow.
Ich muss daran denken *(= ich darf nicht vergessen)*, morgen diese Karte einzuwerfen.

I've **stopped** talking to Rob. We had a fight.
Ich habe aufgehört, mit Rob zu reden. / Ich rede nicht mehr mit Rob. ...
I **stopped** to talk to Jo. We chatted for a while.
Ich hielt an, um mit Jo zu reden. ...

I can't open the door. – **Try** kicking it.
... Probier mal, dagegen zu treten.
I **tried** to kick the door open and hurt myself.
Ich versuchte/bemühte mich, die Tür aufzutreten ...

◂ **3** Nach ***forget, remember, stop, try*** kann entweder ein Gerundium oder ein *to*-Infinitiv stehen, aber mit unterschiedlicher Bedeutung:

– ***forget doing*** *sth.*	vergessen, dass/wie man etwas *(in der Vergangenheit)* getan hat
forget to do *sth.*	vergessen, etwas zu tun
– ***remember doing*** *sth.*	sich daran erinnern, dass man etwas *(in der Vergangenheit)* getan hat
remember to do *sth.*	daran denken, etwas zu tun
– ***stop doing*** *sth.*	aufhören, etwas zu tun
stop to do *sth.*	anhalten, um etwas *(anderes)* zu tun
– ***try doing*** *sth.*	etwas (aus)probieren
try to do *sth.*	versuchen/sich bemühen, etwas zu tun

2.2 REVISION The gerund after prepositions

Boots are made for walking. ... zum Wandern
In future, don't use my mobile without asking.
... ohne zu fragen

I'm very **keen** on playing rugby.
Ich spiele leidenschaftlich gern Rugby.
You're just not **used** to working hard.
Du bist es einfach nicht gewohnt, hart zu arbeiten.

Is there any **hope** of winning the final match?
Besteht Hoffnung, das Endspiel zu gewinnen?
What are his **reasons** for leaving school?
Was sind die Gründe dafür, dass er die Schule verlässt?

Sue **is talking** about moving to London.
Sue redet davon, nach London zu ziehen.
I don't **feel** like going out tonight. Do you?
Ich habe keine Lust, heute Abend auszugehen. Und du?

Nach einer Präposition *(by, for, of, without, ...)* muss ein Verb als Gerundium stehen.

Adjektiv/Nomen/Verb + Präposition + Gerundium:

– *(to) be*	***good/bad at*** ***interested in*** ***keen on*** ***sick/tired of*** ***used to***	***doing*** *sth.*	**Adjektiv + Präposition**
– *the*	***advantage of*** ***chance of*** ***hope of*** ***reason for***	***doing*** *sth.*	**Nomen + Präposition**
– *(to)*	***dream of*** ***feel like*** ***talk about*** ***think of***	***doing*** *sth.*	**Verb + Präposition**

GF 3 Participles

▸ *pp. 158–161*

3.1 REVISION Participle forms

Present participle *(-ing)*:

work → **working** try → **trying**
dance → **dancing** plan → **planning**

◂ Das **Partizip Präsens** *(present participle)* bildet man durch Anhängen von ***-ing*** an den Infinitiv. Beachte die Besonderheiten bei der Schreibung.

Past participle, regular verbs *(-ed)*:

work → **worked** try → **tried**
dance → **danced** plan → **planned**

◂ Das **Partizip Perfekt** *(past participle)* eines regelmäßigen Verbs wird durch Anhängen von ***-ed*** an den Infinitiv gebildet. Beachte auch hier die Besonderheiten bei der Schreibung.

Past participle, irregular verbs:

build → **built** make → **made**
teach → **taught** write → **written**

Unregelmäßige Verben haben eigene *past participle*-Formen, die man einzeln lernen muss.

3.2 REVISION Participle clauses instead of relative clauses

Partizipialsätze können Relativsätze verkürzen und werden daher oft anstelle von Relativsätzen verwendet.

The girl talking **to Leo** is my sister.
(The girl who is talking to Leo ...)
The man driving **the red car** didn't stop.
(The man who was driving the red car ...)

◂ Das ***present participle*** entspricht einem Relativpronomen + Verb im **Aktiv**: *is talking; was driving.*

We often buy strawberries grown **in California**.
(... strawberries which were grown ...)

◂ Das ***past participle*** entspricht einem Relativpronomen + Verb im **Passiv**: *were grown.*

3.3 The present participle after certain verbs

Verb of perception + object + present participle

		Verb	Object	Present participle	
1	I	heard	people	shouting.	
2	Rob	saw	two men	running	out of the bank.
3	Sue	noticed	some men	getting	into a blue car.
4	We	watched	the car	driving	down the street.

Mit einem **Verb der Wahrnehmung + Objekt + Partizip Präsens** sagt man, dass man etwas wahrnimmt, das gerade im Verlauf ist.

Verben der Wahrnehmung sind *feel, hear, listen to, notice, see, smell, watch.*

1 Ich hörte Leute schreien.
2 Rob sah zwei Männer aus der Bank laufen.
3 Sue bemerkte, wie/dass einige Männer in ein blaues Auto stiegen.
4 Wir beobachteten, wie das Auto die Straße hinunterfuhr.

Im Deutschen verwendet man einen Infinitiv (1, 2) oder einen Nebensatz mit „wie“ oder „dass“ (3, 4).

3.4 Participle clauses instead of adverbial clauses

Time

Looking **up**, I saw some small coconuts.
(When I looked up, I saw some small coconuts.)
Als ich aufschaute, sah ich ein paar kleine Kokosnüsse.

Arriving **in Mumbai**, I started to look for a room.
(When I arrived in Mumbai, ...)
Als ich in Mumbai ankam, ...

Asked **to turn down his MP3 player**, the boy started to shout at the bus driver. (When he was asked to turn down ...)
Als er gebeten wurde, seinen MP3-Spieler leiser zu stellen, ...

Partizipialsätze können **Nebensätze der Zeit** oder **des Grundes** verkürzen.

Solche Partizipialsätze gehen oft dem Hauptsatz voran. Sie sind **typisch für das geschriebene Englisch**.

In gesprochenem Englisch werden meist adverbiale Nebensätze bevorzugt.

Reason

Feeling **tired,** I went up to my room.
(Because/Since I felt tired, ...)
Weil/Da ich mich müde fühlte, ...
Warned **by his wife,** the man was able to escape.
(Because he was warned by his wife, ...)
Von seiner Frau gewarnt, ... / Weil er ... gewarnt wurde, ...

***Having* + past participle**

1 Having passed **his exams,** Mike applied for a job.
(After he had passed his exams, ...)
Nachdem Mike seine Prüfungen bestanden hatte, ...

2 Having been **to Italy twice,** we decided to go to Spain.
(Because/Since we had been to Italy twice, ...)
Da wir schon zweimal in Italien gewesen waren, ...

Not having seen **the film,** I bought the DVD.
(Because/Since I hadn't seen the film, ...)
Da ich den Film nicht gesehen hatte, ...

Partizipialsätze mit ***having* + Partizip Perfekt** drücken immer **Vorzeitigkeit** aus.

Partizipialsätze mit ***having* + Partizip Perfekt** entsprechen

1 einem adverbialen Nebensatz der **Zeit**, meist mit *after* eingeleitet,

2 einem adverbialen Nebensatz des **Grundes**.

3.5 Participle clauses giving additional information

I stood in the queue, waiting **to fill my bucket with water.**
Ich stand in der Schlange und wartete darauf, meinen Eimer mit Wasser zu füllen.

Using **a knife,** he was able to open the door.
Indem er ein Messer benutzte, ...

She ran down the stairs, losing **a shoe.**
..., wobei sie einen Schuh verlor.

Partizipialsätze werden oft verwendet, um Zusatzinformationen zu geben oder die Begleitumstände einer Handlung zu beschreiben. (Meist handelt es sich um zeitgleich oder fast zeitgleich stattfindende Handlungen oder Vorgänge.)

Im Deutschen steht meist ein Hauptsatz mit „und" oder ein Nebensatz mit „indem" oder „wobei".

3.6 Extra Participle clauses with conjunctions

1a **Reading** a really boring book, I fell asleep.
Als/Weil ich ein wirklich langweiliges Buch las, ...

1b When/While **reading** a really boring book, I fell asleep. *or* I fell asleep when/while **reading** a really boring book.

2a I saw a huge black dog while **walking** down the street. *(= I was walking down the street)*
Ich habe einen riesigen schwarzen Hund gesehen, während ich die Straße hinunterging.

2b I saw a huge black dog **walking** down the street. *(= the dog was walking down the street)*
Ich habe gesehen, wie ein riesiger schwarzer Hund die Straße hinunterging.

3a After **having** lunch with his girlfriend's parents, Tom fell asleep.
(= first they had lunch, then he fell asleep)

3b **Having** lunch with his girlfriend's parents, Tom fell asleep.
(= he fell asleep while they were having lunch)

4 Although **asked** to stop by the police, the man drove on.
You will have to wait outside until **asked** to enter.

◂ Nicht immer ist eindeutig zu erkennen, ob ein Partizipialsatz einem Nebensatz der Zeit oder einem Nebensatz des Grundes entspricht (Satz **1a**).
Erst durch die Konjunktion ***when*** oder ***while*** wird deutlich, dass der Satz **zeitlich** zu verstehen ist (**1b**).

◂ Oft gibt es große Bedeutungsunterschiede, je nachdem, ob der Partizipialsatz mit oder ohne Konjunktion verwendet wird – vergleiche **2a** mit **2b** und **3a** mit **3b**.

She saw an elephant while cycling along the road.

She saw an elephant cycling along the road.

◂ Partizipialsätze können auch durch andere Konjunktionen eingeleitet werden, z.B. durch ***although, until, if, before.***

1 LISTENING Summer vacation
1 B; *2* B; *3* C; *4* C; *5* B; *6* B

2 LISTENING A day in the life of ...
a) Why bushfires start
b) *1* F; *2* T; *3* F; *4* T; *5* F; *6* T; *7* T; *8* F; *9* T; *10* F; *11* F; *12* T

3 READING Sydney for everyone
a) Sydney's sights
b) Opening times, Sights information
c) *1* T; *2* F; *3* N; *4* T; *5* F; *6* N; *7* T; *8* F; *9* F; *10* N; *11* F; *12* T; *13* T; *14* N; *15* T

4a) WRITING A blog
Hi, friends!
Yesterday I arrived in this most fantastic city–Sydney! Today was our first day of sightseeing. It was pretty hot! First we went to see the famous Sydney Harbour Bridge. People were climbing it – but that's not for me! After that we went to The Rocks, that's an interesting part of town with fantastic old buildings. There are souvenir shops and cafés too. We went to the visitor centre and got some tourist brochures and maps.
My parents wanted to see the Opera House, so we went there next. You can take tours, but Dad said we didn't have enough time. In the afternoon we did a boat trip round the harbour and we sailed under the Bridge. That was better than climbing it!
Tomorrow will be a Bondi Beach day, so we'll have to 'slip, slop, slap'.
Log in again tomorrow and hear all my news!

4b) WRITING A summary
The story is about Nina, her brother David and two friends who drive to Kakadu National Park to celebrate Nina's birthday. On the way they argue about the danger of saltwater crocodiles for tourists. David thinks they should be really careful because park rangers cannot give a guarantee for visitor safety, but Nina says David is too scared. That evening they celebrate at the campsite and next morning they leave for Jim Jim Falls. Nina and Mike want to go swimming there. When they are climbing over the rocks, David hurts his foot and can't continue. He is worried because they lose Nina and Mike. Cathy tries to comfort him. When the two come back, Nina is very quiet. At home she tells David about a huge saltie at the falls and how scared she was. She apologizes to David. She knows he was right and she was stupid. She asks him not to tell their parents.

5a) SPEAKING Travelling
1 Hi/Hello. What can you see on the Uluru tours, please?
2 What time does the tour start?
3 How long does the tour take?
4 Are the tourist guides Aborigines?
5 Do we get breakfast on the tour?
6 How much does the tour cost and what is included in the price?
7 I'd like to book the tour for tomorrow, for two adults and two teenagers, please.

5b) SPEAKING Travelling
Picture A shows a scene in the outback with two people, a white camping bus on the right and a small white tent in the foreground on the left. The man is sitting on the front of the bus looking at the sky, and the woman is sitting on the camping chair. The sky is bright red, so maybe the sun is going down. There's nothing in the background, only red earth for miles. There's nothing green, no plants or bushes. The people look very relaxed. Maybe they're tired after a hot day of driving. It seems to be very lonely and quiet, maybe even boring. They're both wearing shorts, so it is probably still hot. They've put up the tent before it gets dark.

5c) SPEAKING Travelling
I think I would prefer a beach holiday in Australia because the outback is maybe good for people who love adventure but not for people who want to have fun on holiday. Maybe the beaches are crowded, but I love swimming and playing ball games on the beach. I would like to learn to surf too. I like going to discos and I would love the evening beach parties. I like sightseeing, museums, theme parks and shopping. I could do all those things on a beach holiday. I could also practise my English and make new friends.

I would like to make a short trip to the outback, maybe just for two or three days. In the outback the scenery is unique, but maybe it gets boring when you see it all day. I would like to meet some Aborigines and talk to them about their culture and their art.
I'm also interested in the animals in the outback. Maybe I could see a dangerous snake or other animals that live there.

6 MEDIATION Berlin tours
Alpha tours – Berlin: tours by bus, bike or on foot, every day; groups – all sizes; modern buses and new bikes; highlights – Brandenburg Gate, Checkpoint Charlie, small part of the Berlin Wall, TV tower, Berlin Cathedral, Charlottenburg Palace and more; tours morning, afternoon and evening, stops and meal included on day tours, guides speak foreign languages, see website for details

Skills Check 2 Lösungen/Musterlösungen

1 LISTENING First day at work

1 B; *2* A; *3* B; *4* A; *5* B; *6* B; *7* C; *8* A

2 READING Jobs

a) Young people describing jobs that they do
b) *1* D; *2* A; *3* B; *4* F; *5* E
c) *1* Nick *2* Sam *3* Lauren *4* Lucy *5* Nick *6* Adam *7* Sam *8* Sam

3 WRITING A formal letter

Dear Mr Sutton
I read your advertisement in the Cornish Daily Post of ... about jobs for German-speaking students in Cornish hotels this summer. I would like to apply, but I have a few questions first:
What kind of work would I have to do? In which towns are your hotels? How many hours do students work each day/week? How much is the pay? How much free time would I have and when? Would accommodation and meals be free?
I already have some work experience in a German hotel kitchen. I am a friendly, reliable person and a good team worker. I would like to work some time abroad and improve my English.
I look forward to hearing from you.
Yours sincerely

4 WRITING Your CV

Individual answer: please check your answer with the CV and CV tips in your student's book on pp. 38–39.

5 WRITING An informal letter

Hi ...!
It was good to hear from you! Thanks for sending the ad about hotel jobs. Yes, I'm very interested! Let me tell you about it.
Well, my parents think that working away from home would be good for me – and for my English – but they want to know more about the jobs. So I've written to the manager. I asked about the kind of work, pay, free time, accommodation, etc. If it sounds OK, I'll apply.
I'd really like to have some work experience in the UK. It would look good on my CV. I might make some new friends and maybe I could visit you in my free time.
But it may not be very exciting. I expect the work will be quite hard, the pay will be terrible and there won't be much free time ...
I'll write again soon and let you know.
Love ...

6a) SPEAKING Jobs and work experience

Picture 1 shows a tourist guide on a London sightseeing bus, telling tourists about the history of the city and its buildings. Maybe the tourists aren't listening to everything he says. I think it's quite a good job because you are mostly outside and you meet a lot of people. But it's the same routine every day, like most jobs. The guide probably says exactly the same things to all his tourist groups, and he does the same tour at the same time every day. He probably feels bored, but he always has to be friendly.

Picture 2 shows office staff working at their computers in a large, open-plan office. They are probably not very happy that they have to share such a large office. It think it's hard to work there when there are so many people in one room. There's always something happening and there's always some background noise, people telephoning, chatting, walking past you, telephones ringing, etc. The workers are never private. Everybody sees and hears what they do – the boss too.
I would prefer the job of the tourist guide because I think it's more relaxing riding around London in a bus than looking at a computer screen all day.

6b) SPEAKING Jobs and work experience

I think work experience is very important. You have to be punctual, reliable, confident and hard-working. You learn skills that are important for the world of work like organisation, telephone skills, team work, maybe new computer skills.
Last year I worked at a petrol station at the weekends. I had to work in the shop too. I liked chatting to the people there, but it was really boring most of the time. I like to be with people.
I haven't got a job at the moment because I have to work hard for school now.
My favourite school subjects are Maths and Physics. They are both subjects that really interest me, and my grades are good.
When I leave school, I'd like to travel abroad and see how other people live. I'd like to go to South America, and some countries in Asia. After that I think I'd like to get a place at university and maybe study Physics. It would be good to go to the UK or the US for a work placement. Then I could really improve my English.

7 MEDIATION Small ads

1 Job in a café: can work three hours morning or afternoon, have to work in kitchen and café preparing vegetables, doing tables, serving ice cream and cakes in garden, good pay
2 Job in hotel (near cathedral): can work part-time or hourly, have to answer phone calls in English and look after English-speaking guests, needn't have experience of hotel work, above average pay
3 Job with American family: have to look after young children, afternoons, don't have to do housework, needn't have a driving licence
4 Job giving English conversation classes to small groups: two hours twice a week mornings, don't have to speak German